Women, Employment and Development
in the Arab World

New Babylon

Studies in the Social Sciences
41

MOUTON PUBLISHERS · BERLIN · NEW YORK · AMSTERDAM

Women, Employment and Development in the Arab World

Edited by
Julinda Abu Nasr,
Nabil F. Khoury
and Henry T. Azzam

This volume was prepared with the assistance of the International Labour Office, the Institute for Women's Studies in the Arab World (Beirut), and the United Nations Fund for Population Activities.

International Labour Organisation
Regional Office for Arab States

Labour and Population Team
Middle East and Mediterranean Region

Beirut University College

Institute for Women's Studies
in the Arab World

MOUTON PUBLISHERS · BERLIN · NEW YORK · AMSTERDAM

Library of Congress Cataloging in Publication Data

Women, employment, and development in the Arab world.
(New Babylon, studies in the social sciences ; 41)
1. Women – Employment – Arab countries – Addresses, essays, lectures. I.
Abu Nasr, Julinda. II. Khoury, Nabil F., 1948-   . III. Azzam, Henry T.,
1948-   IV. Series.
HD68 6.W66 1984   331.4'0917'4927   84-9935
ISBN 90-279-3380-4

Printed on acid free paper   (pH 7, neutral)

Typesetting: Asian Research Service, Hong Kong. Printing: Druckerei Hildebrand,
Berlin. – Binding: Dieter Mikolai, Berlin.

                                                        Printed in Germany.

Contents

Introduction

Over the last decade interest in the role of women in economic development has increased greatly. This interest culminated in the launching of the United Nations Women's Decade in Mexico in 1975. This has resulted in a number of policy recommendations and research priorities, promoting the integration of women in development and suggesting ways in which women contribute to this process.

The Institute for Women's Studies in the Arab World (IWSAW) and the International Labour Organization (ILO), aware of the scarcity of research on the subject, prepared this book to help fill that need. The book, containing the main determinants of women's productivity in some Arab countries, may serve as a reference on Arab women's economic activities. It also provides quantitative and qualitative data that may be helpful to planners, policy makers and researchers.

The volume includes specific profiles of female labour force participation in Lebanon, the Yemen Arab Republic, the Gulf States and Jordan. It also includes a comparative study on sex-role orientation of university students in Kuwait, Egypt and Lebanon and an overview chapter dealing with basic levels and trends in female labour force participation. A set of policy recommendations for more effective integration of Arab women in development is annexed to the present chapter.

All the country profiles present quantitative descriptions of female labour force participation rates by socio-demographic variables with an interpretation of existing trends and major differences between the sexes. It also describes female labour force barriers to their employment and existing policies aimed at promoting their integration in development.

The measurement of female labour force activity is often under-reported in censuses and surveys conducted in the Arab world. This under-reporting is due mainly to definitions adopted leading to arbitrary division of subsistence activities into 'labour force' and 'non labour force' activities. In addition, statistical data on labour force participation are either inaccurate or incomplete in these countries and great care should be taken in the interpretation of such data, particularly in unpaid labour force.[*]

[*]For more information see Anker, R. 'Female Labour Force Participation in Developing Countries: A Critique of Current Definitions and Data Collection Methods', *International Labour Review* (Vol. 122, No. 6, Nov.-Dec. 1983).

2   Introduction

Chapter 1 identifies the basic trends in the integration of women in development. It presents an overview, by economic sector and major occupational group, of the economically active females in the different Arab countries. It is apparent that the agricultural and the service sectors include the vast majority of female workers in the Arab world. The stereotyped female occupations of teaching, nursing, clerical and secreterial jobs attract most of the educated women seeking employment in the region. In education, there has been a notable increase in female enrolment in schools at the different levels and in the ratio of girls to boys. However, the ratio of girls pursuing vocational and technical education is still very low, and laws stressing equality of treatment and opportunity of work for men and women in most Arab countries remain theoretical. To explain the variability in female labour force participation in services and industry among 18 Arab countries, a single equation model, using fertility, illiteracy, and male labour migration rates, was estimated. The results revealed that these socio-economic and demographic factors have an explanatory power of 60 percent, where no such results are available for the agricultural sector.

In Chapter 2 Myntti analyses the role and status of women in the economy and the society of the Yemen Arab Republic. In a country where about 90 percent of the population live in rural areas and where women have little wage employment opportunities, most of them marry at an early age, raise their children, and work in their fields and their households. The reported low labour force participation rates reveal very little of what Yemeni women are doing. They do have major productive roles but very little cash and little say in household decision-making. Myntti stresses that if women are to be encouraged to participate in the development of their country through various channels, efforts must first be made to change their perception of work, and to ease their tasks as wives and mothers. Yemen is now facing a manpower shortage in various sectors and occupations, exacerbated by the out-migration of working-age males to Saudi Arabia. The remittances sent by the emigrants constitute a major source of income to the country. If the development drive is to continue, the government will have to face the formidable task of tapping available women resources in the country and turn them into a productive workforce.

Chapter 3 presents a general overview of the employment opportunities available for women in the four Gulf States of Bahrain, Qatar and the United Arab Emirates. While the socio-economic development in these countries has been growing drastically, the reported female labour force participation rates continue to be low, perhaps the lowest in the region. After exploring the changing status of women in the Gulf States and the underlying social, cultural and economic variables that are bringing about this change, the chapter then analyses the structure of female employment in these four countries, the educational status of women and the effect that women's employment is having on family life in this part of the world.

In Chapter 4, Chamie presents a case study of the employment situation of Lebanese women, using the results of two major national surveys: the 1970 Economically Active Population Survey and the 1971 National Fertility and Family Planning Survey. The study shows that in 1970, approximately nine percent of all women in Lebanon were economically active. The overwhelming majority of women who worked for remuneration were found in professional, administrative, managerial, clerical, agricultural, industrial and service occupations. The vast majority of working women were found in poorly paid, unprestigious and socially acceptable 'female' occupations. Chamie goes on to say that marriage was strongly and negatively related to female labour force participation. Work experience before marriage substantially improved the probability of a women working after marriage, and this was the case for all five major religious groups in Lebanon (both Christian and Muslim). Regardless of the wife's socio-economic background, the proportion that worked after marriage was considerably less than the proportion that worked before marriage.

Chapter 5 presents the characteristics and structure of female labour force participation in Jordan and gives a detailed description of the factors influencing the participation of women in development. The study shows that participation rates in Jordan remain comparatively low in spite of the rising trend experienced during the past two decades. The low level of female participation could be attributed to a spectrum of cultural, religious, demographic and economic factors. The study shows that there exists considerable scope of increasing the participation of Jordanian women in economic activity. Higher levels of female participation would help in reducing the currently high dependency burden and contribute towards raising household living standards. At the same time, by ensuring the provision of appropriate vocational and technical training to the increasing female workforce, the country could seek to overcome certain skill shortages it has been increasingly faced with, particularly as a result of migration of workers to the oil-rich Gulf States.

In the last chapter, the authors present the findings of a study measuring attitudes towards the role of women as perceived by both male and female university students in institutions of higher learning in the Arab World. The findings show that Arab university students are in a transitional stage, half way between traditionalism and non-traditionalism, and that females are significantly less traditional than males. Some structural variables were found to affect significantly the sex-role attitudes of the students. Father's education in Kuwait and mother's work experience in Egypt were significantly related to sex-role attitudes in the case of males, whereas mother's education was the only variable that had a significant effect on females in Lebanon and Kuwait.

The subject of women, employment and development in the Arab World is both complex and intricate and demands more research than is presently available. However, the following are a few recommendations of the many avenues that need to be explored, while trying to integrate women in the process of economic development.

(1) Detailed information on the scope and determinants of women's work is needed where special attention is given to the measurement of household based labour. There is a need to study the effect of migration (both internal and international) of the male labour force on the work and life conditions of women. Surveys should be designed to acquire pertinent information on socio-economic and demographic indicators affecting the employment of women as well as women's own perception of work, and society's attitudes towards women's work.

(2) Studies of women in rural areas are urgently needed. Of special interest would be studies on the role of rural housewives in decision making within the family. This would help design policies to enhance the role and status of rural women and increase the productivity of the agricultural sector.

(3) In the urban sector, studies are needed to identify employment and recruitment policies and sex discrimination practices in various types of private and public enterprises, employment and training opportunities available for women, modes of production in the formal and informal sector, structure of female employment and underemployment, income levels, and others. Supportive policies and extension activities should be designed to encourage women to enter new occupations besides the traditional stereo-typed ones. Incentives should be provided for women to turn to areas of commodity production, in addition to services. Means and ways to rally the support of the national leadership for the role played by women in the development process of the country should also be considered. The mass media may be utilized to project a positive image of the working woman.

(4) Specific feasibility studies should be undertaken to assess new work opportunities for women (e.g. part-time jobs in urban areas, cottage industries and handcrafts). Supportive services are also needed to relieve women of some domestic chores assigned to them (e.g. child care centers, appropriate maternal, child and health services centers in urban and rural areas).

The findings and conclusions in this book could be considered an attempt to pinpoint the important role that women should play in the development of Arab countries. More in-depth research is needed to achieve a better understanding of the needs for changing attitudes and practices and introducing policy action for the effective integration of women in the process of growth and development.

Chapter 1

An Overview of Arab Women in Population, Employment and Economic Development

H. Azzam, J. Abu Nasr and I. Lorfing

In spite of the region's common culture, it is not possible to talk about the 'Arab woman' since there are sharp disparities among the countries. However, there are some common denominators, such as language, cultural heritage and the Islamic religion, a religion which encompasses a social, legal and moral code of behaviour. The majority of the population in the Arab countries (93 percent) are Moslems and are subject to the provisions of Islamic law, the Sharia. Even in countries where civil law is enforced, the Sharia, derived from the religious text of the Koran, remains the main source of legislation in the Arab countries.

The pace of socio-economic changes occurring in the region varies among and within the countries. These changes, however, 'are selective rather than general and constitute a modification rather than an abandonment of established patterns' (Prothro and Diab, 1974: 206). Indices of the uneven pace of change are reflected in the variability of literacy levels, fertility rates, labour force participation rates and legal status of women.

Rapid transformations are most noticeable in the economic sector, while social changes in general and those concerning the role and status of women in particular lag behind. Economic change may affect women's education and employment, but available research indicates a limited relationship between per capita gross national product and women's attainment in education and employment. Elizabeth White points out that 'poor Moslem States such as Turkey and Tunisia have reformed many laws affecting women and encouraged female education, while some of the wealthier countries, such as Libya and Saudi Arabia, have introduced few or no reforms and report low education achievement of women' (White, 78: 64). White goes on to say that although Islamic laws do not prohibit female education and participation in productive activities, restrictive civil laws hinder her education and employment. Therefore, to understand the state of women's economic participation in a certain society, one has to look at that society's value system, demographic characteristics, economic structure and legal system.

Value System

One of the key values in Arab society determining male-female relationships is that of honor (*ird/sharaf*). In this respect Patai states (1976: 120)

'While honor in its non-sexual, general connotation is termed 'sharaf', the specific kind of honor that is connected with women and depends on their proper conduct is called 'ird'. 'Sharaf' is something flexible: depending on a man's behavior, way of talking and acting, his 'sharaf' can be acquired, augmented, diminished, lost, regained, and so on. In contrast, 'ird' is a rigid concept: every women has her ascribed 'ird'; she is born with it and grows up with it; she cannot augment it because it is something absolute, but it is her duty to preserve it. A sexual offense on her part, however slight, causes her 'ird' to be lost; it cannot be regained.

Family honor depends mainly on the conformity of the female members to the norms and values related to sexual conduct known as the 'modesty code' (Antoun, 1968). To protect female modesty, several measures have been taken, such as the segregation of the sexes, veiling, strict parental surveillance, early marriages, female circumcision and rigid sex-role socialization. Severe restrictions on females' behaviour have confined their activities to their domestic role, have restricted their educational opportunities, thus placing the main responsibility for their economic support on the males in the kinship structure. Therefore, women's participation in non-agricultural or paid labour carries with it a social stigma, and gainful employment is not perceived as part of their role (Youssef, 1978). However, in cases of economic need, women have assumed a provider role. In recent years, the rigid stand against women's employment has been relaxing. Employment statistics show that more women, especially the young and single, are entering the labour force in jobs accepted traditionally as benefiting women, namely, teaching, nursing and services (El Messiri, 1978; Lorfing et al., 1980; Beck and Keddie, 1978; Zurayk, 1978).

A survey conducted in Kuwait by Al Thakib (1975) to assess societal attitudes towards the education and employment of women, found that 96 percent of the respondents were in favour of women's education up to the secondary level. With respect to employment, the majority (90 percent) indicated their approval of women working in government agencies, preferably in teaching, because it provides minimal chances of interaction between the sexes. When assigning priorities between home and job, home was given first priority.

Another study conducted in Lebanon, to evaluate home-based employment programs for young Lebanese rural women (ECWA, 1978a), revealed that 60 percent of the trainees were satisfied with home-based employment and rejected the idea of taking jobs outside their homes and villages. The only occupations specified as acceptable by those willing to work outside their homes were: teaching, nursing and secretarial work.

In Jordan, Abu Jaber et al. (1977) report that the majority of the single women they interviewed planned to quit their jobs after getting married, while 44 percent of the married women stated their desire to leave after having children. The most common reason given was the refusal of husbands to give a hand in housework and the inability of women to reconcile home duties and paid employment.

Statistical data from Egypt, Syria, Lebanon and Tunisia report higher participation rates for single women in the age group 20-24, where the proportion of single women is high; the ratio of participation rates of married women to single women is about 1:4, compared to 1:2 in France or even 1:1 in Bulgaria (United Nations, 1968). These figures indicate that women, at least in some Arab countries, tend to drop out of the labour force after getting married, unless they face a pressing economic need (Lorfing and Abu Nasr, 1980).

Demographic Characteristics

The demographic structure of these countries is characterized by the youthfulness of the population, since the portion aged 15 or less accounts for over 48 percent of the total population. High fertility rates are still prevalent among the majority of Arab States (Zurayk, 1979) which may be attributed to three long-existing factors: the high value given to having a large family, high illiteracy rates, and early marriage (Youssef, 1978).

Studies conducted in Egypt (Schultz, 1972) and in thirteen Moslem countries (Youssef, 1978) confirm that there is an inverse relationship between fertility and level of education, with a positive relationship between education and female activity rate in non-agricultural work. However, a certain level of educational attainment is necessary before a noticeable drop in fertility rate occurs (Tabbarah, 1976). This could explain the uniformly high levels of fertility in the Arab countries, where educational attainment of females is still considered to be generally low.

Table 1: Percentage illiterate of male and female populations 15 years and over in selected Arab countries.

Country	Year	Male	Female
Bahrain	1965	63.9	81.8
	1975	42.0	64.6
Egypt	1966	52.0	79.0
	1975	43.2	71.0
Iraq	1965	64.4	87.2
	1975	58.5	82.8
Jordan	1961	49.9	84.8
	1976	19.0	45.7
Kuwait	1970	36.6	58.1
	1975	32.0	52.0
Lebanon	1970	25.1	47.9
	1975	20.0	44.0
Oman	1975	65.0	98.0
People's Democratic Republic of Yemen	1973	51.2	91.3
Qatar	1975	65.0	98.0
Syria	1962	46.5	83.2
	1975	34.0	76.0
United Arab Emirates	1968	73.0	91.1
	1975	41.6	61.9
Yemen Arab Republic	1975	75.5	98.4

Source: (1) United Nations, *Demographic Yearbook*, 1971.
(2) ECWA, *Demographic and Related Socio-Economic Data Sheets for Countries of the Economic Commission for Western Asia*, Beirut, 1978.

Despite the fact that female illiteracy rates have decreased considerably with the advance of education for girls, they are still high in almost all Arab countries, particularly in countries where education for girls is somewhat recent, as in Oman, Qatar, and the two Yemens (Table 1). One should keep in mind, however, that these rates have been inflated by the lack of education in the older age groups. Considering the younger generation of females we find that the enrolment of girls in schools is increasing in all Arab countries and their percentage of the total student body is rising (Table 2).

Table 2: Evolution of the percentage of girls out of total enrolment by education level in the different Arab countries.

Country	Year	Primary	Secondary	Higher Education
Algeria	1968	37.5	29.2	22.5 (a)
	1975	39.8	33.7	23.4
Bahrain	1968	42.0	38.2	50.3
	1974	43.7	47.1	49.9
Egypt	1968	38.4	31.3	23.2 (c)
	1974	38.0	33.2	29.1
Iraq	1968	29.4	25.6	24.0
	1974	32.4	28.7	29.2
Jordan	1968	42.8	30.2	25.7
	1974	46.1	39.8	33.5
Kuwait	1968	43.8	41.0	46.3
	1974	45.5	45.1	60.5
Libya	1966	29.0	13.0	9.4
	1974	45.4	30.6	15.8
Morocco	1968	32.5	25.7	14.5
	1975	35.9	(b)	18.5
Qatar	1968	43.6	26.7	(b)
	1974	47.9	42.7	(b)
Saudi Arabia	1968	28.1	14.2	5.5
	1974	35.7	29.8	14.8
Sudan	1967	32.6	23.4	10.7
	1974	32.9	29.4	17.1
Syria	1968	34.1	24.2	17.0
	1974	39.2	30.4	21.2
Tunisia	1967	36.7	(b)	18.5
	1975	39.0	32.5	25.5
Yemen (A.R.)	1967	7.0	(b)	(b)
	1974	9.8	9.1	10.7
Yemen (P.D.R.)	1967	20.1	21.5	(b)
	1974	30.3	20.9	18.2
Lebanon	1968	45.5	38.1	21.5 (d)
	1972	46.3	(b)	24.8

(a) Figure for 1973. (b) Data not available. (c) Figure for 1967. (d) Figure for 1971.
Source: United Nations, *Statistical Yearbook,* 1976, 1970.

Although the pattern is changing in some Arab countries, seclusion of women has been the greatest single obstacle to female education. Today, laws and decrees in nearly all Arab states provide equal educational opportunities for both sexes; however, the number of schools for boys exceeds that for girls, and very few are coeducational. Textbooks used reinforce traditional attitudes towards the role of women in society and females are shown conforming to the expected domestic roles (Kallab et al., 1982; Kallab, 1983).

The expansion of primary education differs from one Arab country to another, but the inequality between the educational opportunities available to boys and girls, and between urban and rural areas, is common to the whole region. The inability to get girls to the primary schools, even where attendance is compulsory, is particularly acute in rural areas (UNESCO, 1977a). Nevertheless, primary enrolment has increased considerably. In 1973, nearly half of all primary students in Bahrain, Jordan, Kuwait, Lebanon and Qatar were girls. The country having the lowest proportion of female primary students was the Yemen Arab Republic (Table 2).

Secondary school enrolment of girls has increased at a much slower pace than that of the primary school enrolment, reflecting the persistent tradition of early marriage for girls and the preference for the education of boys. In all the Arab countries, the percentage of girls in secondary education rose from 30 percent in 1970-71 to 33 percent in 1975-76 (Table 3).

Table 3: Evolution of students percentage by educational level and by sex in the Arab countries, 1970-1975.

| | 1970 | | 1975 | |
	Boys	Girls	Boys	Girls
Primary	64	36	62	38
Secondary	70	30	67	33
Higher Education	76	24	72	28
Total	66	34	64	36

Source: UNESCO, 1977. *Recent Quantative Trends and Projections Concerning Enrolment in Education in the Arab Countries.* Conference of Ministers of Education and those responsible for Economic Planning in the Arab States, U.A.E.

At the higher educational level, the proportion of female students increased from 24 percent in 1970-71 to 28 percent in 1975-76 for the Arab countries as a whole (Table 3). Specifically, it ranged from 11 percent in Yemen Arab Republic to 60 percent in Kuwait (Table 2).

Vocational training for girls is still under-developed, and educational opportunities available to women are limited by the attitudes of a conservative society, which deems only certain activities appropriate for women to pursue outside the traditional roles of marriage and childbearing. At best 4-15 percent of all girls in the Arab region have had access to vocational or technical education, and such training was confined to sewing, teaching, nursing and typing. In 1967, the Bahrain Vocational Training College did not have any females, whereas by 1976, women comprised nearly 85 percent of total trainees. Similarly, in the Yemen Arab Republic (YAR), by 1975 nearly 61 percent of the students in teacher training centres were girls, while in Jordan the female percentage in teacher training programs reached 55 percent in 1977 (ECWA, 1978).

The work potential of Arab women has increased with education since women's participation in the labour force and education are interlinked. Education in general has improved the employment opportunities for women and has encouraged more female mobility in the search for employment. It is assumed to have increased the aspirations of women in certain sectors of society for higher income and better standards of living. Moreover, it has weakened the restrictive barriers of traditions and increased the propensity of women to join the labour force. Nevertheless, if women are to play a greater part in productive work, social attitudes, work and educational opportunities, as well as supportive services will have to change.

In addition to education, type of employment and attitudes of employers towards women's participation in the labour force are factors affecting fertility levels and female activity. According to Standing, the type of female employment has a significant impact on their rates of participation. If the opportunity cost of inactivity is low, such as jobs for which parts of entry and re-entry to employment are lax (e.g. various forms of self-employment: sewing, farm work, cottage industry, work in the urban informal sector in general), the opportunity cost of having children will also be low. On the other hand, any interruption of employment for women in 'career' jobs will involve a reduction both in the expected lifetime earnings and in the possibilities of promotion due to seniority. Women in 'career' jobs tend to have fewer children and closer spacing of children. An interruption of employment due to pregnancy and delivery may mean a long wait before a job can be obtained (Standing, 1978).

Furthermore, high fertility rates tend to reduce female economic activity in an indirect way. In societies where large families are the norm and the marriage age is rather low, as in the Arab countries, employers are reluctant to hire married women. They also tend to discriminate against employing unmarried women because the probability of females leaving their jobs after the apprenticeship or training period is far higher than that of males (Richards, 1980).

Another prominent demographic characteristic of the Arab countries today is urban living, with the changes it entails in social organization. A substantial portion of the population in most Arab countries reside in urban areas (Table 4).

Table 4: Percent of total population living in urban areas in selected Arab countries, 1975.

Country	Urban
Bahrain	80.1
Egypt	43.7
Iraq	63.7
Jordan	56.1
Kuwait	88.6
Lebanon	65.0
Oman	5.4
Qatar	88.0
Saudi Arabia	20.8
Syria	46.2
United Arab Emirates	83.9
Yemen Arab Republic	8.9
Yemen Democratic Republic	33.3

Source: ECWA, *Demographic and Related Socio-Economic Data Sheets for Countries of the Economic Commission of Western Asia*, Beirut, 1978.

Female members of families migrating from rural areas tend to accept employment in low-paying jobs of the formal sectors (especially in what urban dwellers consider menial or low status work), or even take up self employment in various activities in the informal sector (AID, 1979). In the oil-producing countries, on the other hand, female employment is sharply reduced after migration from rural to urban areas due to stronger restrictive attitudes towards the employment of women. Knauerhase (1976) observes in his study of 430 farms in Saudi Arabia that when the family moves into the city, women, representing 26 percent of farm workforce, drop out of the labour force since they are not allowed to take a job outside the house.

Another feature of the Arab countries is the recent and massive interregional migration from labour surplus countries such as Jordan, Egypt, Lebanon, Syria, and the Yemen Arab Republic to better-paying jobs in the oil-rich states of the region. Men usually migrate without their wives or female relatives. This migratory trend has created labour shortages in agriculture and in the job labour markets of the sending countries. The agricultural sector is increasingly becoming dependent on its female resources and new job vacancies are being created in the services and industrial sectors that may be filled by women (AID, 1979). In Yemen, for example, women are increasingly taking over activities that, until very recently, were male dominated (Myntti, 1979).

Structure of the Economy

The evolution of the Arab economies from agricultural to their present relatively modern form has been accompanied by changes in the sectoral distribution of their labour force. In Egypt, Lebanon, Syria, Tunisia and Morocco, this evolution began taking shape in the early 1940s, whereas in most other countries, especially the oil countries, the process has begun more recently.

Although agriculture is still a major labour-absorbing sector in countries like Egypt, Syria, Morocco, Sudan and the Yemen Arab Republic, there has been a steady growth in the employment share of the tertiary sector. At the same time, significant changes are occurring in industry and in the service, as reflected in the growing displacement of handicrafts by manufacturing and of the individual workers by companies. The emergence and expansion of new skilled services (educational, health, office work, etc.), and the growth of the oil sector, generating huge capital surpluses to be channeled into development projects, have had, and continue to have, a decisive influence on women's participation in the labour force.

Economic development, modernization and diversification have produced new employment opportunities and improved conditions of work, which, in turn, have stimulated an increased participation of women in the labour force. For the relatively well-educated women, the sectors most affected by the improved conditions are the services (teaching, health, welfare), commercial and industrial undertakings, and public administration. These are the sectors in which women's participation has increased most strikingly in more developed Arab countries (Zurayk, 1979).

In the agrarian Arab countries, women are mostly productive in agriculture, handicrafts and personal services (domestic service, needle work, etc.). Since these occupations are not skill-specific, they are compatible with the prevailing low educational level; moreover, they can generally be carried out within the home by unpaid family workers. This type of work is not included in the labour force figures and partly explains the low female participation rates in those countries.

Legal System

To ensure equality of rights for all citizens in political, economic and social life, and to eliminate discriminatory practices against women workers, special provisions have been incorporated in the constitutions of most Arab countries proclaiming that all citizens are equal with regard to rights and duties. The Egyptian National Charter, for example, states that women must be regarded as equal to men and must play a more constructive role in the society, economy and policy (National Council of Lebanese Women, 1974).

The constitution of Yemen stipulates equal legal rights and obligations to both men and women. The Algerian constitution does not merely list the rights of women but also stresses their responsibilities. It places women on equal footing with men in all spheres of economic and social life. The Libyan Constitutional Proclamation grants every citizen the right to work. The word 'citizen' applies to men and women alike, both being considered equal (National Council of Lebanese Women, 1974).

The Lebanese and Jordanian constitutions guarantee equal working and educational opportunities to all citizens with no discrimination by sex. The Syrian constitution stipulates that the state shall provide women with all the opportunities that would enhance their position and allow them to play a more active role in political, social, cultural and economic life (National Council of Lebanese Women, 1974; Moughaizel, 1979).

In countries where labour legislations have been fully implemented the working conditions of women have much improved. For example, working women are safeguarded against accidents and are entitled to a maternity leave of at least twelve weeks with full or partial payment of salary; moreover, working mothers are entitled to a nursing break during working hours.

Besides maternity protection for which there is a widely recognized need, many countries have protective legal provisions applying exclusively to women; among others are the prohibition of underground work, restriction of female employment in certain occupations regarded as dangerous or harmful, and the prohibition of night work.

Table 5: Comparative schedule regarding various aspects of maternity protection in selected Arab countries.

Sources	Duration of Maternity Leave	Before Delivery	After Delivery	Wages Payable During Leave	Payable Grants (Bonus)	Medical and Delivery Expenses	Sick Leave due to Delivery	Nursing Hours (Breast Feeding)	Nurseries
ILO Conventions	12 weeks	Unspecified	6 weeks	2/3 of salary		Covered by medical insurance on national legislation	To be specified by national legislation	Convention No. 103 Regarding nursing hours	Nurseries to be established by employers
ALO Conventions	7 weeks	Unspecified	5 weeks	Full salary		Medical care and treatment			
1. Bahrain	6 weeks	Unspecified	Unspecified	No pay					
2. Egypt	50 days	Unspecified	40 obligatory days	70% of intial wage					
3. United Arab Emirates	1½ months	Unspecified	Unspecified	No pay					
4. Iraq	10 weeks	1 month	6 obligatory weeks	Full salary			Maximum of 9 months in total	2 periods of ½ an hour each	In establishments employing women
5. Jordan	6 weeks	3 weeks	3 obligatory weeks	½ pay			Sick leave	3 feedings	In establishments employing women

contd.

Table 5 (contd.)

Sources	Duration of Maternity Leave	Before Delivery	After Delivery	Wages Payable During Leave	Payable Grants (Bonus)	Medical and Delivery Expenses	Sick Leave due to Delivery	Nursing Hours (Breast Feeding)	Nurseries
6. Kuwait	70 days	30 days	40 days	Full salary			Continuous or discontinuous 100 days with no pay		
7. Lebanon	40 days	Unspecified	30 obligatory days	Full salary					
8. Libya	50 days	Unspecified	30 obligatory days	Half pay by social Insurance	Maternity grant of 25 Dinars	Medical care before, during & after delivery	A total of 3 months, 50% of salary	One hour daily for 18 months	Institution with 50 or more female employees
9. Oman	6 weeks	Unspecified	Unspecified	No pay			Sick leave		
10. Saudi Arabia	10 weeks	4 weeks	6 weeks	Half pay 50% of salary		Medical and delivery expenses	A maximum of 6 months	One hour daily	Institution with 50 or more female employees
11. Sudan	8 weeks	4 weeks	4 weeks	Full salary				One hour daily for one year	

contd.

Table 5 (contd.)

Sources	Duration of Maternity Leave	Before Delivery	After Delivery	Wages Payable During Leave	Payable Grants (Bonus)	Medical and Delivery Expenses	Sick Leave due to Delivery	Nursing Hours (Breast Feeding)	Nurseries
12. Syrian Arab Republic	60 days	Unspecified	40 days obligatory	Full salary			A total of 6 months as a maximum	2 periods of half an hour each for 18 months	For establishments employing a minimum of 100 employees
13. Tunisia	30 days	Unspecified	Unspecified	Half salary			Renewable leave of 15 days for 12 weeks	2 periods half an hour each for 19 months	
14. Yemen Arab Republic	70 days	Unspecified	40 days obligatory	70% pay					

Source: Arab Labour Organisation, *Committee for Working Arab Women: First Session Documents*, Tunisia, 1974.

To date, a number of the International Labour Organisation's conventions relating to employment of women and protection of motherhood have not been ratified by all Arab countries (Table 6); For example, six Arab countries have not yet ratified convention number 100 on equal remuneration for men and women doing similar jobs, whereas eleven countries have not ratified convention number 118 on equality of treatment in social security matters.

Although most Arab constitutions proclaim that all citizens are equal in rights and duties and stress equal treatment and opportunity in work for men and women (National Council of Lebanese Women, 1974), these policies have not been fully implemented. Working Arab women still face porblems similar to the problems of working women in the rest of the world. Equal remuneration is not applied in many jobs and professions, and there are fewer opportunities opened to them (Newland, 1980; Richards, 1980; Lorfing and Abu Nasr, 1980). The double burden imposed on women, namely, domestic responsibilities and employment aggravated by the lack of social supportive facilities (nurseries, cooperatives, etc.), still hinder their participation in remunerated economic activities (Michel, 1970; Lorfing and Abu Nasr, 1980).

Female Labour Force Participation in the Arab World

Having looked at the Arab Society's value system, demographic characteristics, economic structure and legal system, let us now look at the female labour force participation in these societies. Despite the slight increase in female labour force participation rates over the last decade (Table 7), the average activity rate does not exceed 27.1 percent, a rate lower than the average activity rates in other developing areas, 41.7 percent in Asia and 39.9 percent in Africa (UNESCO, 1977a).

Table 8 provides standardized estimates of female population and activity rates of the different Arab countries for the year 1975. The percentage of economically active females to the total female population ranges from 1.9 percent in Algeria to 22.8 percent in Somalia. The high activity rate in Somalia is due to the active participation of females among the nomads who constitute close to 70 percent of the population. In general, it seems that Arab women play a larger role in economic activities in those countries which are predominantly rural. Female labour in agriculture is acceptable as long as it is confined to the family farms, and considered an extension of their domestic responsibilities. In 1975, urban female activity rates in Sudan and People's Democratic Republic of Yemen (PDRY) were 7 percent and 5

Table 6: Ratification of ILO conventions by the Arab countries regarding women's conditions (As of January 1st, 1979).

Countries	3	4	41	45	81	89	100	103	111	118	122	127	129	135	Total	ILO Members Since
Algeria	X	–	–	–	X	X	X	–	X	–	X	X	–	–	8	1962
Bahrain	–	–	–	–	–	–	–	–	–	–	–	–	–	–	0	1977
Egypt	–	–	–	X	X	X	X	–	X	–	–	–	–	–	6	1936
United Arab Emirates	–	–	–	–	–	–	–	–	–	–	–	–	–	–	0	1972
Iraq	–	–	–	–	X	X	X	!	X	X	X	–	–	X	8	1932
Jordan	–	–	–	–	X	–	X	–	X	X	X	–	–	–	6	1956
Kuwait	–	–	–	X	X	X	–	–	X	–	–	X	–	–	4	1961
Lebanon	–	–	–	X	X	X	X	–	X	–	X	X	–	–	8	1948
Libya	X	–	–	X	X	X	–	X	X	X	X	–	–	–	9	1952
Morcco	–	X	X	X	X	–	–	–	X	–	–	–	–	–	6	1956
Qatar	–	–	–	–	X	–	X	–	X	–	–	–	–	–	3	1972
Saudi Arabia	–	–	–	X	X	X	X	–	X	X	X	–	–	–	7	1976
Sudan	–	–	–	–	X	X	X	–	X	X	X	–	X	–	5	1956
Syria	–	–	–	X	X	X	X	–	X	X	X	–	–	X	9	1947
Tunisia	–	–	–	X	X	X	X	–	X	X	X	X	–	–	9	1956
Yemen	–	–	–	–	X	–	X	–	X	–	–	–	–	–	4	1965
Democratic Yemen	–	–	–	–	–	–	–	–	–	–	–	–	–	–	0	1969

X = Ratified.
– = Not ratified yet.

contd.

Table 6 (contd.)

1	–	Convention No. 3	Regarding women's employment before and after delivery.
	–	Convention No. 4	Night work for women.
	–	Convention No. 41	Night work of women (reviewed in 1934).
	–	Convention No. 45	Work for women in mines in all categories.
	–	Convention No. 81	Inspection of work in the industrial and commercial sectors.
	–	Convention No. 89	Night work for women in certain industries (reviewed in 1948).
	–	Convention No. 100	Equal remunerations between women and men for similar jobs.
	–	Convention No. 103	Concerning maternity protection (revised 1952).
	–	Convention No. 111	Sex discrimination regarding employment and progressions.
	–	Convention No. 118	Equality of treatment in social security matters.
	–	Convention No. 122	Employment policy.
	–	Convention No. 127	Maximum weights which may be carried, drawn or pushed by women.
	–	Convention No. 129	Labour inspection in agriculture (1969).
	–	Convention No. 135	Workers' representatives (1971).

Table 7: Evolution of labour force participation in selected Arab countries.

Country	Year	Male	Female	Total	% Female in Economically Active Population*
Algeria	1966	42.2	1.8	21.7	4.3
	1975	43.4	1.9	22.3	4.3
Egypt	1966	51.2	4.2	27.9	7.5
	1972	50.8	4.0	27.6	7.2
	1975	50.4	4.1	27.5	7.5
Jordan	1961	42.4	2.6	22.9	5.7
	1971	43.1	2.6	23.1	5.6
	1975	44.4	3.0	24.2	6.0
Kuwait	1961	47.4	0.4	29.7	0.5
	1970	53.0	5.2	32.4	6.9
	1975	47.9	5.1	28.5	8.1
Libya	1964	46.6	2.7	25.6	5.1
	1975	47.4	2.7	25.9	5.0
Morocco	1960	50.1	5.9	28.0	10.6
	1971	44.5	8.0	26.3	15.2
	1975	44.4	7.9	26.1	15.1
Syria	1960	46.0	5.4	26.3	10.1
	1970	42.7	5.5	24.8	10.8
	1975	45.2	6.0	26.6	11.2

Source: International Labour Office, *Yearbook of Labour Statistics,* Geneva, 1966 and 1978.
*Because of the nature of subsistence activities and family farming which is widespread in the Arab world, female labour force activities are often under-reported. These figures, therefore, tend to be under-estimated.

Table 8: Economically active females in Arab countries 1975.

Country	Female Population (in Thousands)	Active Females (in Thousands)	Percentage of active Females to Total Female Population	Percentage of active Females to Total Female Population Aged 15 years and above	Percentage of Active Female to Total Active Population
Algeria	8,532	159	1.9	3.2	4.3
Bahrain[a]	121	3.249	2.7	2.7	5.4
Egypt	18,598	795	4.3	6.2	7.6
Iraq	5,441	118	2.2	2.0	4.2
Jordan	1,311	39	3.0	2.8	6.0
Kuwait	492	26	5.3	5.1	8.1
Lebanon	1,425	137	9.6	8.9	18.4
Libya	1,085	29	2.7	4.5	5.0
Mauritania	649	17	2.6	4.0	4.3
Morocco	8,758	691	7.9	13.1	15.1
Qatar	68	1.8	2.7	...	2.2
Saudi Arabia	4,431	113	2.6	2.4	4.7
Somalia	1,603	365	22.8	37.5	29.4
Sudan	9,039	608	6.7	11.1	10.6
Syria	3,549	212	6.0	5.0	11.2
Tunisia	2,912	116	4.0	6.4	8.5
U.A.E.[a]	171	9.961	5.8	5.7	3.4
Y.A.R.	3,295	81	2.5	2.3	4.3
P.D.R.Y.	821	22	2.7	2.6	5.0

Source: Unless otherwise specified: ILO, *Labour Force Estimates and Projections, 1950-2000,* Vols. I and II, Geneva, 1977.
a ECWA, *Statistical Abstract of the Region of the Economic Commission for Western Asia,* Second Issue: Part I, Beirut, 1978.

percent, respectively, while the activity rates of rural women were 27 percent for Sudan and 12 percent for Yemen (Azzam and Shaw, 1980).

The distribution of economically active females by broad economic sectors (agriculture, industry and service) in the Arab countries is reported in Table 9. The figures show that a good portion of the active female population is still working in the agricultural sector (88 percent in Sudan, 87 percent in Yemen Arab Republic, 79 percent in PDRY and 66 percent in Saudi Arabia). If the country has a significant urban sector, (e.g. Lebanon, Egypt, Kuwait, Qatar, United Arab Emirates (UAE) or Bahrain), women tend to work mainly in community or in social and personal services (Table 9). Data revealed that 97 percent of the total active females in Bahrain are engaged in services, compared to 96 percent in the UAE, 99 percent in Kuwait and 56 percent in Lebanon.

Table 9: Percentage distribution of economically active female population by sector in the Arab countries.

Sector	Bahrain	Egypt	Iraq	Jordan	Kuwait	Lebanon
	1971b	1975	1975	1971	1975b	1975
Agriculture, hunting, forestry and fishing	0.2	16.1	26.7	23.5	0.2	21.9
Mining and quarrying	a	0.2	a	a	0.1	a
Manufacturing	2.4	10.4	11.4	8.8	0.3	20.8
Electricity, Gas and Water	0.1	0.6	0.9	a	0.1	1.2
Construction	0.4	0.6	a	a	a	a
Wholesale and retail trade, restaurants and hotels	3.7	7.4	10.5	14.7	0.4	19.6
Transport, storage and communication	2.6	2.2	10.5	5.9	3.6	a
Finance, insurance, real estate and business services	2.7	1.9	21.9	47.1	95.3	4.0
Community, social and personal services	85.9	40.9				32.1
Activity not well defined	2.0	19.7	18.1	a	a	0.4
Total	100.0	100.0	100.0	100.0	100.0	100.0

Source: Unless otherwise specified – ECWA, *Statistical Abstract of the Region of the Economic Commission for Western Asia* – Second Issue, Part I Beirut, 1978.

– ILO, *Yearbook of Labour Statistics*, Geneva, 1978.

Table 9 (contd.)

Libya	Qatar	Saudi Arabia	Syria	Tunisia	United Arab Emirates	Yemen Arab Republic	People's Democratic Republic of Yemen	Sudan
1973	1975	1975	1975	1975	1975	1975	1976	1976d
38.5	a	66.4	80.9	25.1	0.4	87.2	79.5	87.9
0.9			0.1	0.2	2.0	a	a	2.9
4.6	a	11.5	6.2	45.2	1.1	1.3	3.2	
0.3			0.2	0.2	0.2	a	0.1	0.1
0.6			0.3	0.4	2.5	0.3	a	0.1
1.5			1.0	2.6	4.6	2.7	0.4	1.9
1.0			0.4	1.1	3.3	0.1	0.1	0.3
1.4	100	21.1	0.3	0.7	5.7	0.1	0.1	c
50.4			9.8	17.3	80.2	8.3	7.8	5.9
0.8			0.8	7.2	a	a	8.8	0.9
100.0	100.0	100.0	100.0	100.0	100.0	100.0	100.0	100.0

Notes:
a Negligible or zero.
b Rates are for nationals.
c Include in the rates for sector No. 6: Wholesale and Retail Trade, Restaurants and Hotels.
d Source: Aisha Abdallah. 'A study of population and rural manpower in the Sudan'. (Paper presented at the Seminar on Population, employment and migration in the Arab Gulf States – Arab Planning Institute, Kuwait, 1978 (in Arabic).

While the majority of female workers are engaged in agriculture and service jobs, the other sectors have very low female participation rates (Table 9). With the exception of Lebanon and Tunisia, where manufacturing absorbs

Table 10: Distribution of economically active females by professional groups in selected Arab countries (percentages).

Country		Total Active Females	Professional Group						
			0-1	2	3	4	5	6	7-9
Algeria	A	99,100	18.3	1.2	10.5	1.5	29.3	23.4	15.7
(1966)	B		20.9	6.0	11.6	1.3	13.3	1.8	3.5
Bahrain	A	3,249	51.6	2.2	12.3	1.4	28.7	0.2	2.3
(1971)	B		34.8	6.9	7.8	0.9	9.4	0.1	0.3
Egypt	A	631,700	22.4	1.5	16.9	5.4	11.3	15.2	7.4
(1975)	B		25.1	8.8	18.7	5.4	9.2	2.2	2.4
Kuwait	A	35,206	40.2	0.1	12.1	0.9	44.8		0.8
(1975)	B		33.8	1.5	11.2	1.3	20.2	0.2	0.3
Lebanon	A	99,135	20.2	0.2	9.8	3.1	21.4	21.4	18.6
(1970)	B		37.8	2.1	21.6	4.6	33.7	20.9	10.0
Libya	A	35,900	28.8	0.1	4.8	0.5	22.3	38.1	5.4
(1973)	B		19.2	0.5	4.5	0.6	10.0	12.2	1.0
Morocco	A	533,200	4.5	5.2		1.9	23.4	42.8	22.2
(1971)	B		15.0	23.3		4.5	38.1	11.2	15.5
Syria	A	170,644	24.1	9.7		0.8	2.7	36.6	21.0
(1976)	B		29.8	11.4		0.8	9.7	10.8	5.2
Tunisia	A	262,300	6.1	0.1	6.5	1.0	10.2	26.4	49.7
(1975)	B		22.2	4.9	20.0	3.5	28.4	13.2	23.9

Notes:
* Negligible or zero.
A Percentage distribution of economically active females by professional groups.
B Percentage distribution of economically active females in the total active population of each professional group.
Professional Groups
0-1: Professional, technical and related workers.
  2: Administrative and managerial workers.
  3: Clerical and related workers.
  4: Sales workers.
  5: Service workers.
  6: Agricultural, animal husbandry and forestry workers, fishermen and hunters.
7-9: Production and related workers, transport equipment, operators and labourers.
Source: ILO, *Yearbook of Labour Statistics,*1977.

21 percent and 45 percent, respectively, female employment in such sectors as transport, storage and communication, construction, electricity, gas and water, mining and quarrying is reported to be very low for all countries.

The percentage distribution of economically active females by professional groups in selected Arab countries is given in Table 10. The percentage of economically active females belonging to group 0-1 (professional, technical and related workers varies considerably among the countries of the region. While this percentage is 4.5 percent in Morocco for the base year 1971, in Bahrain, it is as high as 51.6 percent for the same base year, compared to 22.4 percent in Egypt and 20.2 percent in Lebanon. Considering the percentage of working women in this professional group out of the total active population (males and females), the figures show more homogeneity across countries. It is, for example, 25 percent in Egypt, 33.8 percent in Kuwait, 29.8 percent in Syria and 22.2 percent in Tunisia, all for the base year 1975.

Arab females in professional group 2 (administrative and managerial) represent a very small percentage of the active female population, rarely higher than 1 percent, while the percentage of working females to total active population of this group is slightly higher and ranges from 0.5 percent for Libya to 8 percent for Egypt.

On the average, 11 percent of the total active female population in the Arab world belong to group 3 (clerical and related workers), and a much lower percentage, around 2 percent, to group 4 (sales workers). For group 5 (service workers), the percentage of working women out of the total female active population rises considerably. It is, for example, around 44.8 percent for Kuwait, 29.3 percent for Algeria, 28.7 percent for Bahrian, 11.3 percent for Egypt and 21.4 percent for Lebanon.

The percentage of total active females in group 6 (agriculture, animal husbandry and forestry) varies considerably across countries of the region. Whereas, the percentage is negligible in Kuwait and Bahrain (less than 1 percent, it is as high as 42.8 percent in Morocco, 38.1 percent in Libya, 36.6 percent in Syria and 26.4 percent in Tunisia.

With the exception of Lebanon, Syria, Morocco and Tunisia, the percentage of economically active women belonging to the groups 7-9 (production and related workers, transport equipment, operators and labourers) is rather low. It ranges from 0.8 percent in Kuwait, to 49.7 percent in Tunisia with 2.3 percent in Bahrain, 5.4 percent in Libya, 18.6 percent in Lebanon, 21 percent in Syria and 22.2 percent in Morocco. The oil-rich countries of the region tend to be more conservative towards having women working in manufacturing sectors than do other countries of the region. Furthermore countries at a higher level of industrialization tend to have a higher percentage of their active female labour force engaged in groups 7-9 than do countries at lower levels of industrialization and development.

To conclude, the professional groups that absorb most of the working females in the Arab world are those of the social services, public administration, agriculture and personal services. Because of differences in the patterns of female employment, this generalization cannot be made for every Arab country. Nevertheless, one may reasonably assume that the average Arab woman would seek employment opportunities in these female stereotyped occupations where she is accepted and for which she is trained.

In this chapter we have discussed determinants of female labour force participation in the Arab World, an area on which little has been done. A similation equation model which had been attempted by one of the authors of this chapter (Azzam, 1979), using 1970 as the base year whereby female labour force participation, crude birth rate (as a measure for fertility), infant mortality rate and secondary school enrolment rate, were determined endogenously in the model. The exogenous variables reflected existing socio-economic and demographic conditions in the Arab countries and included such factors as per capita income, illiteracy rates, level of urbanization and out-migration.

For this study, Azzam estimated a single equation model using a cross-section of eighteen Arab countries, with 1975 as the base year. Female labour force participation (LFPR) is hypothesized as a function of crude birth rate (CBR); percentage of migrants in the labour force (M/L), which is positive for countries experiencing outflow of migrants and negative for countries experiencing migrant inflow; female illiteracy rate (Illit$_F$), which represents the mother's educational level; and a dummy variable D. D takes the value of 1 for countries where there are minimal restrictions on female activities; otherwise it takes the value of zero.

The crude birth rate is included as an independent variable because it is a significant factor in determining the supply of female labour. The childcare burden, associated with high birth rates, acts as a depressant on women joining the labour force and, therefore, (CBR) is expected to be negatively associated with (LFPR).

As previously indicated the labour surplus countries of Jordan, Egypt, Lebanon, Syria and Yemen Arab Republic have been experiencing a flow of out-migrants to the oil-rich countries of the region. The migratory trend has created labour shortages in the markets of the sending countries and a lot of job vacancies are being filled with the female members of the indigenous labour force. The percentage of migrants in the labour force (M/L) is, therefore, expected to be positively related to (LFPR). The larger the percentage of out-migrants to the labour force, the larger will be the demand for female activities to replace the departing migrants.

Female illiteracy rate should be negatively related to (LFPR). The higher the literacy level of females, the higher the opportunity cost of inactivity and the higher the participation rate of females in the labour force.

Table 11: Data used in regression analysis.

Country	$LFPR_F$	M/L Out Migration	CBR	EA_F	Ag.	Ag_F	Y/N	$Illit_F$	$LFPR_{SIF}$	D
Algeria	4.3	0.02	48.7	19	55.4	22.20	803	85.4	13.1	1
Bahrain	9.9	- 9.42	45.0	61	6.5	0.10	2,350	64.6	9.4	0
Egypt	7.6	4.26	35.5	21	47.8	16.10	310	71.0	20.5	1
Iraq	4.2	- 0.52	41.6	20	56.2	26.90	1,155	82.8	11.6	1
Jordan	12.5	42.09	50.0	32	32.7	38.70	419	45.7	12.8	1
Kuwait	11.6	-47.96	51.1	61	2.5	0.06	11,431	52.0	11.4	0
Lebanon	18.4	6.64	33.0	52	16.9	21.90	1,080	44.0	31.3	1
Libya	5.0	-55.92	45.0	23	22.8	37.70	4,618	53.0	13.4	0
Morocco	15.1	0.07	46.0	15	54.0	41.30	440	88.2	39.0	1
Oman	2.0	16.70	50.0	6	64.5	67.20	2,139	98.0	6.0	0
Qatar	2.2	-18.52	50.0	51	3.0	0.01	7,240	98.0	3.3	0
Saudi Arabia	4.7	-29.36	48.9	10	66.1	66.40	3,538	90.0	4.2	1
Sudan	10.6	0.89	47.8	7	79.5	85.50	258	76.0	23.8	1
Syria	21.1	4.85	47.8	23	48.8	79.80	560	87.0	14.1	1
Tunisia	8.5	2.79	39.9	32	32.4	22.90	728	61.9	28.8	0
U.A.E.	3.3	-21.23	50.0	15	4.6	0.40	13,500	98.4	6.2	0
Y.A.R.	12.1	25.54	48.9	1	77.2	87.20	180	91.3	6.7	0
P.D.R.Y.	18.5	19.65	45.4	6	49.1	79.50	122		5.8	0

Definitions and Sources

1. $LFPR_F$ Female Labour Force Participation Rate; the percentage of women in the Total Active Population.
    Source   ECWA, *Demographic and Related Socio-economic Data Sheets for Countries of the Economic Commission for Western Asia*: Beirut, 1978.
    BIT, *La Participation Des Femmes a l'Activité Economique et leurs Conditions de Travail Dans les Pays d'Afrique*: Genève, 1978.

contd.

Table 11 (contd.)

2.	CBR	Crude Birth Rate.
	Source	ECWA, *Demographic and Related Socio-economic Data Sheets for Countries of the Economic Commission for Western Asia*: Beirut, 1978.
		U.N., *Statistical Yearbook*: New York, 1976.
3.	EA_F	Female Educational Attainment, the percentage of females enrolled in school, of the age group 12-17.
	Source	UNESCO, *Recent Quantitative Trends and Projections Concerning Enrolment in Education in the Arab Countries*: Paris, 1977.
4.	Ag.	The Percentage of the Total Economically Active Population in Agriculture.
	Source	ILO, *Yearbook of Labour Statistics*, Geneva, 1977 and 1978.
		FAO, *Production Yearbook*, vol. 31, 1977.
5.	Ag_F	Percentage of the Female Active Population in Agriculture.
	Source	ECWA, *Demographic and Related Socio-economic Data Sheets for Countries of the Economic Commission for Western Asia*: Beirut, 1978.
		ILO, *Yearbook of Labour Statistics*: Geneva, 1978.
6.	Y/N	Per capita income, in U.S. Dollars.
	Source	ECWA, *Demographic and Related Socio-economic Data Sheets for Countries of the Economic Commission for Western Asia*: Beirut, 1978.
		UN, *Yearbook of National Accounts Statistics*, Vol. II: 1977.
7.	$Illit_F$	Female Illiteracy Rate.
	Source	ECWA, *Demographic and Related Socio-economic Data Sheets for Countries of the Economic Commission for Western Asia*: Beirut, 1978.
		UNESCO, *Statistical Yearbook*: 1976.
	also	ECWA, *Statistical Abstract of the Region of the Economic Commission for Western Asia*, 2nd Issue, Part I; Beirut, 1978.
8.	Out-Migration	$\dfrac{\% \text{ out-migrants}}{\text{Labour Force}}$ when figure is (1) then: $\dfrac{\% \text{ in-migrants}}{\text{Labour Force}}$
	Source	ECWA: *Statistical Abstract of the Region of the Economic Commission for Western Asia*, 2nd Issue, Part I: Beirut, 1978.
		ILO, *Yearbook of Labour Statistics*: Geneva, 1978.
9.	$LFPR_{SI}$	*Percentage female in the Total Labour Force, engaged in Industry and Services Activities.*
	Source	ECWA; *Statistical Abstract of the Region of the Economic Commission for Western Asia*, Beirut.
		ILO, *Labour Force Estimates and Projections: 1950-2000*; Vol. I and II, Geneva, 1977.
10.	D	1 In the Arab Countries where we have minimum restrictions on female employment.
		0 Otherwise.

The dummy variable is expected to be positively related to (LFPR). Where we have little or no restrictions on women's activities these activities tend to be higher.

It is perhaps worthwhile noting that the choice of explanatory variables in the model was not only restricted to the aforementioned four variables. Other variables (e.g. degree of urbanization, educational attainment, per capita income,) were included at one point but later dropped from the regression due to their poor explanatory powers.

The data used to estimate the model are given in Table 11. A major limitation of the study is the lack of reliable demographic data in the region. Besides, comparing labour force statistics cross-sectionally is particularly difficult because of differences in definitions and classifications among the different Arab countries.

The estimated regression is:

$$LFPR = 20.431 - 0.085 \, CBR + 0.094 \, M/L - 0.092 \, Illit_F + 0.887 \, D$$
$$R^2 = 0.030.$$

The estimated co-efficients have the expected sign; and the independent variables explain 30 percent of the variation in LFPR.

In the Arab countries, the work of women in traditional sectors is undertaken mostly as part of family labour, and, therefore, is rarely considered as labour force participation. While some countries of the region consider certain female activities in the traditional sector as paid employment and would, therefore, include the working female in the labour force, other countries consider similar activities as domestic, and thus are excluded from labour force statistics. The inconsistency arising in female labour force participation figures cannot be simply ignored or downscaled in a cross-sectional analysis study. By redefining the dependent variable of the model to include only females working in the services and industry sectors, we would expect to be in a better position to use cross-sectional data in explaining variations in female labour force participation.

Using the same explanatory variables as before, i.e. crude birth rate (CBR), percentage of migrants in the labour force (M/L), female illiteracy rates ($Illit_F$), the dummy variable D, and the dependent variable, now defined as the percentage of females in the total labour force that are engaged in industry and services activities, over total labour force including women in agriculture the following regression was estimated.

$$LFPR_{SI} = 32.751 - 0.544 \, CBR + 0.078 \, M/L - 0.002 \, Illit_F + 13.198 \, D$$
$$R^2 = 0.61$$

The estimated co-efficients have the expected sign. This regression has a higher explanatory power than the one presented above and may be considered a better fit.

The results confirm the main hypothesis that female labour force participation in the Arab world depends on the underlying socio-economic and demographic factors. Differentiating between female-remunerated activities in services and industrial sectors, and more general familial-aid activities in the agricultural sectors has increased our ability to explain variations in female labour force participation across the countries of the region. Until more reliable data are made available on female participation in agriculture, one would be better off resorting to female participation in secondary and tertiary sectors to explain variations in female employment across countries.

Another important result of the regression analysis is the significant negative relationship between fertility and female labour force participation. A high fertility rate would act as a depressant on female labour force participation.

Conclusion

In this overview, we have tried to present a profile of Arab women in population, employment and economic development. It has been apparent through our discussion that female labour force participation rates in the Arab countries are low in general with marked differences among countries. Literacy rates, fertility levels, legal reforms in civil and labour laws, and degrees of urbanization, were found to carry a strong explanatory power of female economic participation levels. However, the prevailing value system embedded in the 'modesty code' seems to have a strong impact that is visible but difficult to measure. Strict adherence to this code resulting in the seclusion of women in some countries of the region is reflected in the low literacy rates, low employment levels in the modern sector, and few changes in restrictive laws affecting women's status. Even in countries where there is some relaxation of this code, female labour force participation is still low compared to other developing countries. This may be due to the assurance of economic support within the kinship structure which minimizes financial pressures and makes it possible for many women to stay economically inactive.

This trend is changing in some of the countries (Lebanon, Tunisia, Egypt, Syria) due to inflation and economic pressure in the city, which induces women to seek employment. Although urbanization and industrialization have increased educational and job opportunities for women, nevertheless, female employment rates remain relatively low.

Arab countries are still in the early stages of the process of economic development and could use the contribution of every member of society

to speed up the process. Women are the Arab world's unutilized and un-
recognized human reserve. Policy measures should be designed at all levels
to enhance female labour force participation.

Integrating women in economic development does not mean a repudiation
of all aspects of the traditional role of Arab women; nor does it mean a blind
imitation of developed societies. The value of proper childcare and strong
family ties may continue to rank high on the priority list of Arab societies,
and women would continue to be the key members in the functioning of the
family network. It is very important for anyone involved in development
planning of Arab society to be aware of the hidden economic contribution
of women and their potential working force.

Bibliography

Abd-Allah, A., 1978. *A Study of Population and Rural Manpower in the Sudan.* A paper
presented at the seminar on population, employment and migration in the Arab Gulf
States: Kuwait (In Arabic).

Abdel-Basit, A., 1975. 'On Working Women in Kuwait and the Arab Gulf'. In Cultural
and Social Committee for Women. *Studies on the Conditions of Women in Kuwait
and the Arab Gulf.* Kuwait: Fahd Marzouk Press (In Arabic).

Albrain, A., 1974. *The Veil of the Moslem Women in the Koran and Sunna.* Cairo:
Salafiya Edition (In Arabic).

Abu-Jaber, K., 1977. Abdel-Ati, S. and Ghoraibeh, F., 1977. *Conditions of some Working Women in Jordan.* Paper presented at the seminar of population, employment and
development. Amman.

Abu-Nasr, J. and Lorfing, I., 1981. 'Socialization of Preschool Children in Lebanon',
In Monograph 4, *Social and Moral Issues of Children and Youth in Lebanon.* Beirut:
Institute for Women's Studies in the Arab World, Beirut University College.

Abu-Reida, M., 1975. 'Women in Islam'. In *Cultural and Social Committee for Women,
Studies on the Conditions of Women in Kuwait and the Arab Gulf.* Kuwait: Fahd
Marzouk Press (In Arabic).

Agency for International Development, Office of Women in Development. 1980. *Women
in International Migration.* Washington, D.C.

Al-Khammash, S., 1973. *Arab Women and Traditional Society.* Beirut: Dar Al Hakika
(In Arabic).

Al-Matwi, A., 1960. *Women in the True Islam.* Tunisia: Tunisian Company for Art (In
Arabic).

Al-Thakib, F.T., 1975. 'Women in Contemporary Society'. In Cultural and Social Committee for Women, *Studies on the Conditions of Women in Kuwait and the Arab
Gulf.* Kuwait: Fahd Marzouk Press (In Arabic).

Anker, R., 1976. *An Analysis of Fertility Differentials in Developing Countries.* World
employment programme research working paper. Geneva: ILO, Mimeographed.

Antoun, R.T., 1968. 'On the Modesty of Women in Arab Muslim Villages: A Study in
the Accommodation of Tradition'. *American Anthropologist 72,* 3.

Arab Labour Organisation. 1974. Committee for Working Arab Women, First Session:
Documents: *Tunisia* (In Arabic).

Azzam, H., 1979. 'Analysis of Fertility and Labour Force Differentials in the Arab World', *Population Bulletin of ECWA* 15.

Azzam, H. and Shaw R., 1980. *Population, Labour Force and Rural Employment in the Five Least-Developed Arab Countries.* Beirut: ILO, Regional Office for Arab States.

Badran, H., 1972. *Arab Women in National Development.* Prepared for the Seminar on Arab Women in National Development: Cairo.

Bakalian, A., 1981. *A Review of the Status of Contemporary Arab Women.* Tunis: The International Planned Parenthood Federation (unpublished).

Barth, P.S., 1968. 'Unemployment and Labour Force Participation'. *Southern Economic Journal* 34, 3.

Beck, L. and Keddie, N. (eds.) 1978. *Women in the Muslim World.* Cambridge Massachussetts: Harvard University Press.

Ben-Porath, Y., 1973. 'Labour Force Participation and the Supply of Labour'. *Journal of Political Economy* 81, 3.

Berger, M., 1962. *The Arab World Today.* New York: Doubleday and Company, Inc.

Bilsborrow, R.E., 1973. *Effects of Economic Dependency on Labour Force Participation Rates in Less-Developed Countries.* A paper presented at the inaugural meeting of the Eastern Economic Association: New York. Mimeographed.

Bindary, A., Baxter, C.B. and Hillingsworth, T.H., 1973. 'Urban-Rural Differences in the Relationship Between Women's Employment and Fertility: A Preliminary Study'. *Journal of Biosocial Science* 5, 2.

Blaug, M., 1974. *Education and Employment Problem in Developing Countries.* Geneva: ILO.

Blaxall, M. and Reagan, B. (eds.), 1976. *Women and the Workplace.* Chicago and London: University of Chicago Press.

Boulding, E., Nuss, S.A. et. al., 1976. *Handbook of International Data on Women.* California: Sage.

Boserup, E., 1970. *Women's Role in Economic Development.* London: Allen and Unwin.

Bourguiba, H., 1965. 'A New Role for Women', In Rivlin, B. and Szyliowicz, J.S. (eds.), *The Contemporary Middle East: Tradition and Innovation.* New York: Random House.

Bowen, W.G. and Finegan, T.A., 1965. 'Labour Force Participation and Unemployment'. In Ross, A.M. (ed.), *Employment Policy and the Labour Market.* Berkeley: University of California Press.

—, 1966. 'Educational Attainment and Labour Force Participation'. *American Economic Review* 65, 2.

El-Calamawy, S., 1969. 'Women Win their Way to Higher Public Posts'. *Times,* July 24.

CEAO, 1974. *Le Status Legal de la Femme Musulmane dans Plusieurs Pays Moyen-Orient.* (Comission Economique Pour l'Asie Occidentale, E/CONF/60.SYM. IV/17.

Chabaud, J., 1970. *The Education and Advancement of Women.* Paris: UNESCO.

Chamie, M., 1977. 'Sexuality and Birth Control Decisions among Lebanese Couples'. *Signs: Women and National Development,* (special issue) 3, 1.

Concepcion, M.B., 1974. 'Female Labour Force Participation and Fertility', *International Labour Review,* 109, 5-6. Geneva: ILO.

El-Daghestani, K., 1965. 'The Evolution of the Moslem Family in Middle Eastern Countries'. In Rivlin, B. and Szyliowicz, J.S. (eds), *The Contemporary Middle East: Tradition and Innovation.* New York: Random House.

Denti, E., 1968. 'Sex-Age Patterns of Labour Force Participation by Urban and Rural Populations'. *International Labour Review* 98, 6.

Djebar, A., 1961. *Women of Islam.* London: Andre Dutsch Limited.

Dodd, P.C., 1968. 'Youth and Women's Emancipation in the United Arab Republic'. *Middle East Journal* 22, 2.

—, 1973. 'Family Honour and the Forces of Change in Arab Society'. *International Journal of Middle East Studies* 4, 1.

ECWA, 1977. *Employment and Development.* A paper presented at the seminar on population, employment and development. Amman.

−, 1978a. *Evaluation of Home Based Employment Programmes for Lebanese Rural Women'* Beirut: Social Development and Human Settlement Division.

−, 1978b. *Technical Cooperation Among Developing Countries and Women's Role in Development in the ECWA Region.* A paper for the workshop on technical cooperation among developing countries and women. Tehran.

−, 1978c. *Demographic and Related Socio-economic Data Sheets for Countries of the Economic Commission for Western Asia.* Beirut.

−, 1978d. *Statistical Abstract of the Region of the Economic Commission for Western Asia.* Second Issue, Part I. Beirut.

El-Assad, S. and Khalifa, A., 1977. 'Fertility Estimates and Differentials in Jordan, 1972-1976'. *Population Bulletin of the United Nations Economic Commission for Western Asia* 12.

El-Attar, M.E., 1973 'Differential Fertility in the Arab Republic of Egypt'. *Social Biology* 20, 3.

El-Messir, S., 'Self Images of Traditional Urban Women in Cairo'. In Beck, L. and Keddie, N. (eds.), *Women in the Muslim World.* Cambridge. Massachussetts: Harvard University Press.

El Shafei, A.M.N., 'The Current Labour Force Sample Survey in Egypt'. *International Labour Review* 82, 5.

Federici, N., 1968. 'The Effects of Female Employment on Fertility'. In Szabody, E. et al. (eds.), *World Views of Population Problems.* Budapest: Akadeniai Kiado.

Fernea, E., 1976. *A Street in Marrakesh.* New York: Anchor Books.

Fernea, E.W. and Bezirgan, B.Q., 1977. *Middle Eastern Muslim Women Speak.* Austin: University of Texas Press.

Fox, G.L., 1977. 'Nice Girl: Social Control of Women Through a Value Construct'. *Signs: Journal of Women in Culture and Society* 2, 4.

Gendell, M., 1967. 'The Influence of Family Building Activity on Women's Rate of Economic Activity'. In *Migration, Urbanization, Economic Development.* New York: United Nations.

Gordon, D.C., 1968. *Women of Algeria: An Essay on Change.* Cambridge, Massachussetts: Harvard University Press.

Groat, M.J., Workman R.L. and Neal, A.G., 1976. 'Labour Force Participation and Family Formation: A Study of Working Mothers'. *Demography* 31, 1.

Haddad, W., 1978. 'The Legal Provisions Governing the Status of Women in Some Arab Countries'. *Population Bulletin,* United Nations, ECWA 14.

Hauser, P.M., 1972. 'The Work Force in Developing Areas'. In Berg, I. (ed.), *Human Resources and Economic Welfare.* New York: Columbia University Press.

Hunt, A., 1968, *A Survey of Women's Employment.* Government's Social Survey, London: HMSO.

Hussein, A., 1973. 'Status of Women and Family Planning in a Developing Country − Egypt'. In Omran, A.R. (ed.), *Egypt: Population Problems and Prospects.* Chapel Hill: Carolina Population Centre.

International Labour Organisation, 1966. *Yearbook of Labour Statistics.* Geneva: ILO.

−, 1970. *Toward Full Employment.* Geneva: ILO.

−, 1977. *Labour Force Estimates and Projections: 1950-2000,* I and II.

−, 1978. *Yearbook of Labour Statistics.* Geneva: ILO.

Jordan, 1977. *The Population Situation in Iraq, Jordan and Syria.* A paper presented at the seminar on population, employment and development. Amman.

Kallab, I., Abu Nasr, J.and Lorfing, I., 1982. 'Sex-Role Images in Lebanese Text Books'. In Gross, I., Downing, J. and D'Heurle, A. (eds.), *Sex-Role Attitudes and Cultural Change.* Holland: Reidl.

Kallab, I., 1983. *Hiya Tatbukh wa Howa Yakra'a.* (She Cooks, He Reads). Monograph 3. Beirut: Institute for Women's Studies in the Arab World. Beirut University College (In Arabic).

Khan, M., 1972. *Purdah and Polygamy: A Study in the Social Pathology of the Muslim Society.* Peshawar, Pakistan: Sami H. Khan.

Khayyat, A., 1975. *An Islamic Viewpoint on the Concept of Association of Both Sexes and its Rules.* A paper presented at the seminar on the status of women in the Muslim family. Cairo.

Knauerhause, R., 1976. *Social Factors and Labour Market Structure in Saudi Arabia.* Yale Economic Growth Centre. Discussion Paper No. 247.

Lloyd, C.B. (ed.), 1975. *Sex, Discrimination and the Division of Labour.* New York and London: Columbia University Press.

Lorfing, I. and Abu Nasr, J., 1980. 'Lebanese Women, Heads of Households'. In Monograph No. 1, *Women and Work in Lebanon.* Beirut: Institute for Women's Studies in the Arab World, Beirut University College.

Lorfing, I. and Abu Nasr, J., 1980. 'The Female Industrial Worker and the Suburbs of Beirut in 1979'. In Monograph No. I, *Women and Work in Lebanon.* Beirut: Institute for Women's Studies in the Arab World, Beirut University College.

Lutfiyya, A.M., 1970. 'The Family'. In Lutfiyya, A.M. and Churchill, C.W. (eds.), *Readings in Arab Middle Eastern Societies and Cultures.* The Hague: Mouton.

Makhlouf, C., 1979. *Changing Veils.* London: Groom Helm.

McCable, J.L. and Rosenweig, M.R., 1976. 'Female Labour Force Participation, Occupational Choice, and Fertility in Developing Countries'. *Journal of Development Economics* 3,2.

Mernissi, F., 1976. 'The Moslem World: Women Excluded from Development'. In Tinker, I. and Bramsen, M. (eds.), *Women and World Development.* Overseas Development Council.

Michel, A., 1970. *La Sociologie de La Famille.* La-Haye: Mouton.

Mincer, J., 1962. 'Labour Force Participation of Married Women: A Study of Labour Supply'. In Lewis, H.G. (ed.), *Aspects of Labour Economics.* Princeton: Princeton University Press.

–, 1966. 'Labour Force Participation and Unemployment: A Review of Recent Evidence'. In Gordon, R.A. and M.S. (eds.), *Prosperity and Unemployment.* Berkeley; university of California Press.

Mohsen, S.K., 1967. 'The Legal Status of Women among the Awlad 'Ali'. *Anthropological Quarterly* 40, 3.

Moughaizel, L., 1979. *Al Mara'a Fi Al Tachrih al Lubnani.* (The Woman in Lebanese Law). Beirut: Institute for Women's Studies in the Arab World. Beirut University College. (Unpublished).

Myntti, C., 1979. 'Population Process in Rural Yemen: Temporary Emigration, Breast Feeding and Contraception'. *Studies in Family Planning* No. 10: 282-289.

Naji, M.N., 1971. *Labour Force and Employment in Egypt.* New York: Praeger.

Nasif, A., 1978. *Human Resources in Kuwait.* A paper presented at the seminar on population, employment and migration in the Arab Gulf States. Kuwait (In Arabic).

National Council of Lebanese Women. *The Status of Women in Arab Laws.* Beirut.

Newland, K., 1980. *Women, Men and the Division of Labour.* Worldwatch Paper 37.

Papanek, H., 1977. 'Development Planning for Women'. *Signs: Women and National Development* (special issue) 3, 1.

Patai, R. *The Arab Mind.* New York: Charles Scribner's.

Perstiany, J.G., 1965. *Honour and Shame: The Values of Mediterranean Society.* London: Weidenfield and Nicholson.

Pinelli, A., 1971 'Female Labour and Fertility in Relationship to Contrasting Social and Economic Conditions'. *Human Realtions* 24, 6.

Planning Council, Kuwait, 1974. *Annual Statistics of Kuwait.* Kuwait Statistical Center.

Population Reference Bureau, Inc., 1978. *World Data Sheet.* Washington, D.C.

Preston, S.H. and Richards, A.T., 1975. 'The Influence of Women's Work Opportunities on Marriage Rates'. *Demography* 12, 2.

Prothro, E.T., 1961. *Child Rearing in the Lebanon.* Cambridge. Massachussettes: Harvard University Press.

Prothro, E.T. and Diab, L., 1974. *Changing Family Patterns in the Arab East.* Beirut: American University of Beirut.

Research and Population Studies Centre. *The Egyptian Women in 20 years, 1962-1972.* Egypt (In Arabic).

Richards, E., 1980. 'The Employment Status of Women in Lebanon'. In Monograph 1. *Women and Work in Lebanon.* Beirut: Institute for Women's Studies in the Arab World. Beirut University College.

Rosaldo, M. and Lamphere, L., 1974. *Women, Culture and Society.* Stanford: Stanford University Press.

Schneider, J., 1971. 'Of Vigilence and Virgins, Honour, Shame and Access to Resources in Mediterranean Societies'. *Ethnology* 10, 1.

Schultz, T.P., 1972. 'Fertility Patterns and their Determinants in the Arab Middle East'. In Cooper, C.A. and Alexander, S.S. (eds.), *Economic Development and Popualtion Growth in the Middle East.* New York: American Elsevier.

Seward, G.H. and Williamson, R.C., 1970. *Sex Roles in Changing Society.* New York: Random House.

Siddiqi, M.M., 1966. *Women in Islam.* Lahore: The Institute of Islamic Culture.

Shaw, P., 1978. *Is the Arab World Over-Populated? A look at the Five Least Developed Arab Countries.* A paper presented at the seminar on population, employment and development. Amman.

Shea, J.R., Spitz, R.S., Zeller, F.A. et al., 1970. *'Dual Careers: A Longitudinal Study of Labour Market Experience of Women'. Its Manpower Monograph* 21.

Sinha, J.N., 1967. 'Dynamics of Female Participation in Economic Activity in a Developing Economy'. In *Migration, Urbanization, Economic Development.* New York: United Nations.

Sobol, M.G., 1973. 'A Dynamic Analysis of Labour Force Participation of Married Women in Childbearing Age'. *Journal of Human Resources* 8, 4.

Standing, G., 1976. *Female Labour Supply in an Urbanizing Economy.* Geneva: ILO.

–, 1978. *Labour Force Participation and Development.* Geneva: ILO.

Standing, G. and Sheehan, G., 1978. *Labour Force Participation in Low Income Areas: Case Studies.* Geneva: ILO.

Sweet, T.A., 1973. *Women in the Labour Force.* New York: Seminar Press.

Tabbarah, R., 1976. 'Population Education as a Component of Development Policy'. *Studies in Family Planning* 7, 18.

Turnham, D., 1970. *The Employment Problem in Less Developed Countries.* Paris: OECD.

United Nations., 1968. *Demographic Yearbook.* New York: U.N.

–, 1970. *Statistical Yearbook.* New York: U.N.

–, 1971. *Demographic Yearbook.* New York: U.N.

United Nations, 1976. *Statistical Yearbook.* New York: U.N.

UNESCO, 1956. *Compulsory Education in the Arab States.* Amsterdam: Drukkerij Holland N.V.

–, 1970. *Comparative Study of Co-education.* Paris.

–, 1977a. *New Prospects in Education for Development in the Arab Countries.* Conference of Ministers of Education and those Responsible for Economic Planning in the Arab States. Abu Dhabi.

–, 1977b. *Recent Quantitative Trends and Projections Concerning Enrolment in Education in the Arab Countries.* Conference of Ministers of Education and those Responsible for Economic Planning in the Arab States. Abu Dhabi.

Vajrathon, M., 1976. 'Towards Liberating Women: A Communications Perspective'. In Tinker, I. and BoBramsen, M. (eds.), *Women and World Development.* Overseas Development Council.

Van Nieuwenhuijze, C.A., 1971. 'A Category Aside: Woman'. In Van Nieuwenhuijze, C.A. *The Sociology of the Middle East.* Leiden: R.J. Brill.

White, E., 1978. 'Legal Reforms as Indicator of Women's Status in Muslim Nation'. In Beck, L. and Keddie, N. (eds.), *Women in the Muslim World.* Cambridge, Massachussettes: Harvard University Press.

Wilensky, H., 1968. 'Women's Work: Economic Growth, Ideology and Social Structure'. *Industrial Relations* 7.

Woodsmall, R.F., 1956. *The Role of Women, Their Activities and Organizations in Lebanon, Egypt, Iraq, Jordan and Syria.* Vermont: The Elm Tree Press.

Youssef, N.H., 1971. 'Social Structure and the Female Labour Force: The case of Women Workers in Muslim Middle Eastern Countries'. *Demography* 8, 4.

—, 1972. 'Differential Labour Force Participation of Women in Latin America and Middle Eastern Countries: The Influence of Family Characteristics'. *Social Forces* 51, 2.

—, 1973. 'Cultural Ideals, Feminine Behavior and Family Control'. *Comparative Studies in Society and History* 15, 3.

—, 1974. *Women and Work in Developing Societies.* Berkeley: University of California.

—, 1976. 'Women in Development: Urban Life and Labour'. In Tinker, I., and Bramsen, B. (ed.), *Women and World Development.* Overseas Development Council.

—, 1978. 'The Status and Fertility Patterns of Muslim Women'. In Beck, L. and Keddie, N. (eds.), *Women in the Muslim World.* Cambridge, Massachussettes: Harvard University Press.

Yusuf, H.S., 1965. 'In Defence of the Veil'. In Rivlin, B. and Szyliowicz, J.S. (eds.), *The Contemporary Middle East: Tradition and Innovation.* New York: Random House.

Zellner, H., 1972. 'Discrimination Against Women, Occupational Segregation and the Relative Wage'. *American Economic Association Papers and Proceedings* 62, 2.

Zurayk, H., 1977. 'The Effect of Education of Women and Urbanization on Actual and Desired Fertility and on Fertility Control in Lebanon'. *Population Bulletin of the United Nations Economic Commission for Western Asia* 12.

—, 1979. 'The Changing Role of the Arab Women'. *Population Bulletin of the United Nations Economic Commission for Western Asia* 17; 18-31.

Chapter 2

Women, Work, Population and Development in the Yemen Arab Republic

C. Myntti

Yemen is one of the least known and most often misunderstood countries in the Arab World. Occupying the mountainous, densely populated southwest corner of the Arabian Peninsula, it does not share a past of European domination like other countries in the region. Rather, it remained an independent monarchy until 1962, suffered through eight years of civil war, and only in the 1970's has it put civil strife behind it, and gotten on with developing the infrastructure and ideologies of a modern nation state. Apart from the fact that Yemen, or Arabia Felix, was the home of Bilqis, the renowned queen of Saba, little else is known about the rulers, society and the women of contemporary Yemen. Its people are proud and pragmatic. They are predominantly farmers deriving a subsistence from steeply terraced agricultural plots. To many Yemenis, the days of insufferable poverty are vivid memories of recent times. Yet, like other Arab countries, Yemen is indirectly affected by the oil boom; labour migration and workers' remittances afford traditional Yemeni society the material goods and lifestyle of the twentieth century.

Let us begin by looking at Yemen through standard socio-economic indicators. A national census is being planned for 1985. For the time being the most reliable population figures derive from the first national census of 1975. That census enumerated a resident population of about 4.7 million people, 90 percent of whom were rural. The census attests to the norm of small settlements with 34 percent of the population living in settlements of 100 inhabitants or less and 78 percent of the population living in settlements of less than 500 (Swiss, 1977: I-141).

More than half the resident population is female, with the national sex ratio at 91 males per 100 females. This is due to the out-migration of working-age males to Saudi Arabia and other oil-producing states of the Gulf. The most reliable figures put the number of short-term Yemeni migrants abroad at around 500,000, which means that between one-third and one-half of all adult males are out of the country (Swiss, 1978: I-91-94; Steffen and Blanc, 1982: 100).*

The population of Yemen is a young one, with 47 percent younger than 15 years of age. The crude birth rate is high and estimated at 46/1000, though the crude death rate is also high at 22/1000. The natural rate of increase is calculated to be about 2.4 percent per annum, with the high birth rate being offset by the death rate (Swiss, 1978: I-90).

The infant mortality rate remains very high due to poor health and sanitation conditions, and ranges between 155 and 210 per thousand according to various estimates. Life expectancy at birth is not more than 42 years (Swiss, 1978: I-88).

A great part of the Yemeni population is illiterate. The census recorded 75 percent of all males over 10 years of age as not able to read and write, while 98 percent of the females were illiterate. These figures will change as more children enter the formal education system. Despite the growth of the primary school network in the country since the revolution of 1962, in 1976/77 the percentage of pupils in primary school amounted to only 27 percent of the boys and 5 percent of the girls in the age groups of 5-14 years (Swiss, 1978: I-111, 118).

The above demographic, health and literacy statistics rank Yemen among the least developed countries in the world. Economic indicators such as the GNP, however, place Yemen among the fastest growing countries of the world. The per capita GNP has risen from just ever $100 in the early 1970s to $390 in 1976/77 (World Bank, 1979, 1). This rise is not due to the development of an industrial economy or an increase in agricultural production, but, rather, to the inflow of remittances from Yemeni workers abroad. Working age males are, in fact, Yemen's most valuable export.

The out-migration of Yemeni males makes the country as dynamic and different place than it was even a decade ago. Women and their work, the subject of this chapter, must be understood in the context of such dramatic economic and social change brought about in great part by the shortage of male labour, the inflow of remittances and the large amounts of bilateral and multilateral development aid being given to Yemen.

It is not possible to provide in this chapter credible quantitative measures on the extent to which Yemeni women participate in the labour force. Such

---

* There has been considerable controversy over the number of migrant labourers outside Yemen. Demographers argue that if the resident population numbers around 5 million it would be an impossibility to have 1.5 million adult male labourers out of the country. The Confederation of Yemeni Development Associations (CYDA) conducted a census in 1981 to show 1.4 million migrants out of a total population of 8.5 million (CPO, 1982: 37; World Bank, 1979: 14-16.)

measures, which would allow regional and international comparisons, do not exist yet for Yemen. A 1975 manpower survey (Table 1) and the 1975 census (Tables 2, 3) provide only rudimentary statistics on the females employed in the three major cities, Sana's, Ta'iz and Hodeida.

Table 1: Distribution of the female labour force in relation to the total population in YAR by province, 1975. (Absolute figures and percentage)[1]

Province	Total Population	Population 10 years[2] and over	Labour Force	Our of Labour Force
	100.0	66.3	60.6	5.7
Sana'a	418,984	277,970	254,000	23,970
	100.0	75.9	73.2	2.7
Ta'iz	416,399	316,169	304,880	11,289
	100.0	66.2	58.1	8.1
Al-Hodeidah	333,779	220,865	193,847	27,018
	100.0	65.9	64.5	1.4
Ibb	418,992	276,174	270,091	6,083
	100.0	67.8	62.6	5.2
Dhamar	242,933	164,665	152,096	12,569
	100.0	65.7	60.7	5.0
Hajjah	201,905	132,639	122,602	10.037
	100.0	66.7	40.6	26.1
Sa'adah	83,188	55,492	33,833	21,659
	100.0	40.8	30.3	10.5
Al-Mahweet	153,796	62,781	46,599	16,182
	100.0	65.2	63.2	2.0
Al-Beida	87,550	57,057	55,308	1,749
	100.0	60.4	53.0	7.4
Ma'arib	19,589	11,839	10,383	1,456
	100.0	66.3	60.7	5.6
TOTAL	2,377,115	1,575,651	1,443,639	132,012

Source: Yemen Arab Republic, Central Planning Organisation. *Statistical Yearbook, 1979-1980.* Sana'a: July 1981, p. 62.
[1] Percentages are shown in line 1.
[2] Excluding 'not stated' population.

42   C. Myntti

Table 2: Distribution of the male labour force in relation to the total population in YAR by province, 1975. (Absolute figures and percentage)[1]

Province	Total Population	Population 10 years[2] and over	Labour Force	Out of Labour Force
	100.0	63.5	49.2	14.3
Sana'a	400,022	254,016	196,846	57,170
	100.0	58.9	38.2	20.7
Ta'iz	401,377	236,368	153,366	83,002
	100.0	64.5	50.0	14.5
Al-Hodeidah	339,310	218,690	169,589	49,101
	100.0	60.1	44.0	16.1
Ibb	370,528	222,516	162,950	59,566
	100.0	62.1	47.4	14.7
Dhamar	210,955	131,073	99,955	31,118
	100.0	62.6	49.5	13.1
Hajjah	192,921	120,812	95,535	25,277
	100.0	63.7	53.6	10.1
Sa'adah	75,222	47,899	40,334	7,565
	100.0	60.9	48.4	12.5
Al-Mahweet	81,713	49,755	39,583	10,172
	100.0	55.7	40.2	15.5
Al-Beida	71,579	39,867	28,742	11,125
	100.0	57.9	44.4	13.5
Ma'arib	19,496	11,285	8,660	2,625
	100.0	61.6	46.0	15.6
TOTAL	2,163,123	1,332,281	995,560	336,721

Source: Same source as in Table 1.
[1]Percentages are shown in line 1.
[2]Excluding 'not stated' population.

The Yemen data presented here may be useful in ways in which comparative labour force statistics are not, for they call into question some basic assumptions on which most measures of labour force participation rest. For example, the census listed only 9 percent of all Yemeni women as participants in the labour force (they are working for a wage in the urban modern sector). This figure, however, does not begin to tell us anything about the work of the 90 percent of the population in the countryside where agriculture is the primary economic activity, and where some estimates say that women do 75 percent of the work.

Socknat and Sinclair, who have been studying the manpower situation in Yemen since the early 1970s make this comment on the labour force participation statistics from the census (1978: 17):

That 90 percent of females age ten and over were reported to have 'no need to work' is curious given the share of population supported by agricultural economic activity. We suppose that the census enumerators in the YAR had difficulty, as their counterparts do in most LDC's, in making respondents realize that women's chores in the fields count at least as 'unpaid family labour'. We fully appreciate the criticism of labour force definitions developed by males in western industrial societies on the grounds of bias in respect of: (1) western concepts; (2) industrial definitions; and (3) sex.

Thus the question of women and work in Yemen calls attention to the deficiencies of the standard measure of work and the labour force participation rate. For Yemen, the labour force participation rate is useful in as much as it tells us something about the work of a very small number of formally employed city women. It may give us an idea of possible trends in the future and identifies areas of problems. Its apparent value ends there.

For Yemen, the more appropriate first step is an evaluation of the work of women in the traditional sectors, non-formal home-based industry, traditional marketing and agriculture. Taken together, these represent an important area of economic activity in Yemen and underline the importance of the work of women. To exclude these activities would be to take an unfruitful and narrow view of the economy and of the economic roles of women.

A full understanding of the range and intensity of women's work, part and parcel of understanding Yemen's labour force, is vital for development planning in Yemen. Development in Yemen means more than simply an increased participation for women in formal education and the modern sector. It also means the extension of appropriate agricultural technology to women in the countryside. This can be accomplished only after the actual work roles of Yemeni women have been made explicit.

This chapter is divided into two main sections. The first presents some data on women in the urban, modern workforce. This section includes what statistics are available and some tentative explanations as to why they are so low. The second section describes the work of women in the Yemen countryside and how it is changing.

Yemeni Women in the Urban Labour Force

Labour Force Participation Rate
The 1975 census records 3,703 women as economically active in the cities of Sana'a, Ta'iz and Hodeida. This figure represents only women who are employed for wages in the modern work sector and constitutes approximately 4 percent of the urban labour force. Unfortunately, the characterisitcs of

these 3,703 women are not known in any systematic way. The following observations have been made, however, and will have to suffice until more detailed information is available.

Location: Modern sector employment (in schools, hospitals, factories, offices, shops and in services) can be found in Sana'a, Ta'iz and Hodeida. Women in small but increasing numbers may also be engaged in employment in rural market towns such as Ibb, Dhamar, Rida', Turba, Zabid, Mahwit, Hajja, Sa'ada, Jibla and al-Baydha. Some work as teachers in government schools and others as cleaners or nurses in hospitals. Turba, in a progressive region of the southern part of the country, has approximately ten girls teaching in the local school and four working in the hospital.

Education: Any employment which demands education or skills is filled by younger women who have had access to the formal education system or have been educated outside Yemen. It must be remembered that there was no formal education system in the country for girls until after the Revolution of 1962. Prior to that time, only a small number of girls from elite families were taught literacy and religion in private establishments. Even now, if one finds a young woman in her early twenties with education or training above the secondary level, she is likely to have received all or part of her education abroad probably in Aden, Ethiopia or Egypt. Since the opening of Sana'a university in 1974, an increasing number of Yemeni women have been receiving higher education; and this should broaden the participation of women in professional categories. In the academic year 1980-1981, 508 of the total 4519 were female students. Their specializations were as follows: law, 46; arts, 185; science, 64; commerce and economics, 83; education, 130 (CPO, 1982: 219).

Age: The vast majority of females working as teachers or in office jobs are in their late teens or early twenties. They have had some education and training, and often continue working until they marry. This is a very small group of women and since they have some education, they are permitted to work outside their fathers' homes, and are allowed to marry later than most of their peers.

The women involved in industrial production or as cleaners tend to be older and are often divorced or widowed. Usually illiterate, these women are not trained for other work. They may be forced to work in order to support themselves.

Marital Status: The majority of women formally employed outside their homes either have never married, or are divorced or widowed. In her book on Sana'ani women, C. Makhlouf (1977: 17) states that her sample contained 40 upper class women, 11 of whom were employed. Of the 11, three were married, one a widow, four unmarried and three divorced. However, a small but increasing number of university-educated married women are joining the professional ranks of government and the educational system.

Unmarried girls tend to form a young and elite group which has had some education and training, and parental permission to work outside their homes until they marry. Divorced and widowed women tend to work for a wage to support themselves independently or to contribute to the expenses of the household which has absorbed them. In theory, a divorced or widowed woman has the right to be supported by her male kin. In practice, however, most widows and divorcees support themselves or feel morally obliged to contribute to the budget of the extended family.

Children: Married women who have children may be inhibited from taking up employment due to lack of childcare facilities. In many cases, children can be cared for by women of the extended family. A problem arises, however, when kin are not nearby, as is often the case with migrants to the cities.

Babysitting and domestic help are prohibitively expensive in Yemen, and there are only two functioning daycare centers in the entire country. Both in Sana'a, one at the Textile Factory and one established by the Yemen Women's Association. Some mothers are forced to bring their children to work with them, which presents problems both for employers and for children.

Occupational and Employment Status of Women
The two sources of statistical information on the occupations of Yemeni women are the 1975 manpower survey and the 1975 population census.

The Manpower Survey: This survey shows that 1146 Yemeni females were employed in modern sector establishments, with a little over two-third of them employed by government agencies. The ministries of health, education and municipalities engaged most of the female government employees while those women working in private sector establishments were predominantly engaged in unskilled manual tasks.

The Population Census: The data provided by the census are different from those of the manpower survey, but the trends are essentially the same. Table 3 shows a breakdown of the labour force in Sana'a, Ta'iz and Hodeida by occupation. These data have been derived from the 1975 census and number the employed females in the three cities at 3,703 or about 4 percent of the total labour force in the cities (see Tables 1 and 2).

Production labourer: The largest number of females, 1287, are employed in this category, though they constitute only 2.4 percent of the total number employed in production. These women are employed in the few factories which exist in Yemen: textiles in Sana'a, plastics and biscuits in Ta'iz and cigarettes in Hodeida. The women employed in this category are thought to be older, illiterate, of low socio-economic status and often migrants to the cities.

Service workers: This category includes women who sweep the streets in the cities and women who work as cleaners. They number 756 and account

Table 3: Labour force in major cities by occupation and sex, 1975.

Occupation	Sex	Al-Hudaydah	Ta'iz	Sana'a
Professional, technical and related workers	M	1037	1182	1412
	F	238	190	306
Total		1275	1372	1718
Administrative and managerial workers	M	542	390	1903
	F	8	7	26
Total		550	397	1929
Clerical and related workers	M	1531	1221	2878
	F	17	46	128
Total		1548	1267	4006
Sales workers	M	3813	3557	3567
	F	119	117	38
Total		3932	3674	3605
Service workers	M	790	1057	1593
	F	197	266	293
Total		987	1323	1886
Agricultural, animal husbandry and forestry workers, fishermen and hunters	M	522	255	576
	F	95	7	13
Total		617	262	589
Production and related workers, transport equipment operators and labourers. Also 'not-stated'	M	17465	12974	20868
	F	348	191	748
Total		17813	13165	21616
Seeking work for the first time	M	256	570	339
	F	36	256	13
Total		292	826	352
GRAND TOTAL	M	25956	21206	34436
	F	1058	1080	1565
Total		27014	22286	35701

Source: Same as in table 1.

for 18 percent of those employed in this category. The percentage is high in urban areas partly because poor migrant women are often forced to work because of financial necessity, and will take work that other city people are not willing to take. Women who work in this category are often of the *Akhdam* social strata, reputedly of Ethiopian descent.

Professional/technical: The next most significant group, numerically and proportionally, is women employed in the professional and technical category. Numbering 734, they comprise 17 percent of the labour force in this group and consist primarily of school teachers and health personnel. The percentage of women in this category is comparatively high because health and education professions are considered more acceptable and proper for females.

It is noteworthy that women are a significant part of the professional group in Yemen. A shortage of trained men in this category points to the serious problem of lack of professionals, whether male or female in a country which still suffers from the legacy of no formal modern education.

Clerical: In 1975, 191 women were recorded as working in clerical jobs. This represented 2.8 percent of all those employed in office jobs. It appears that employment in this field, more than any other, has changed since 1975. In 1979 several hundred women were working in banks in Sana'a alone, both as typists and as money counters. Many females even those fully veiled, can now be observed in the typing rooms of Government ministries. These jobs pay well and the girls can be segregated into rooms to maintain a decorum of modesty. Typing courses are offered by the National Institute of Public Administration in Sana'a and also by the Yemeni Women's Association.

Managerial/Administrative: There are 41 Yemeni women in managerial or administrative positions according to the 1975 census, which constitutes 1.4 percent of the total in this category. These are predominantly school head-mistresses. While some exceptional women administrators exist in the country, there are not many women with enough education and seniority to hold such posts.

Figures for the next two occupational categories, sales and agriculture, demonstrate the limited application of official statistics to wage employment. Even in urban areas the informal marketing activities of women, as well as their processing and sales of dairy products and poultry, are significant and would not turn up in labour force participation statistics.

Sales: 274 women, or about 2 percent of the total labour force in this category, are listed as working in commerce. If the commercial activities which occur informally at afternoon tea parties among women were included in such figures, the female participation rate would be much higher. Clothes, gold and even foods are often sold at social gatherings of women, but in the privacy of family homes. In many urban markets, women also sell bread, eggs, vegetables and herbs at the side of the road, not in shops.

Agriculture/Animal husbandry, etc: This category appears to be incomplete since only 115 women, or 7 percent of the total, are recorded. In some cases the line between traditional and modern, public and private might have been confused. For example, it is doubtful that women raising chickens for prized *baladi* eggs or women processing milk into *saman* would be counted as 'employed', or indeed as 'labour force participants', despite the fact that they are economically productive and meeting the market demand for traditional products in urban areas.

In summary, the 1975 census statistics show that women and girls in Yemen form 17 percent of the professional category and 18 percent of the service category. The highest numbers of women are working in industrial production, though they are only 2.4 percent of all employees in this category. This demonstrates that women are entering the labour force at the high and low ends of the formal employment spectrum. Younger high status women with some education are entering professional employment, while older lower status women are working in factory and municipality jobs. The figures presented do not include remunerative and non-paid work of women in commerce, animal production and agriculture in either the cities or the countryside.

Barries to Female Employment

Since 1973/74, the shortage of labour in all sectors of the Yemeni economy has been so great that women could have relieved the situation had they been able to step in. Why haven't they?

Changes are occurring fast in Yemen. One of the causes of change is the massive countrywide out-migration and the ensuing labour shortage. In order to fill the employment gaps, the government, rather than training the remaining men, boys and women with the necessary job skills, has imported foreign labour. The Yemeni government has espoused the goal of developing its manpower. However, one sees Sudanese nurses, Egyptian teachers, Pakistani bankers Indian construction workers and Ethiopian office workers in urban Yemen. Yemen is now importing labour as well as exporting it, because much of the Yemeni population cannot be trained quickly enough to meet the demands.

As far as women are concerned, however, their non-participation implies more than lack of training and education. It hinges on culturally-defined attitudes and practices which are common throughout the Middle East: pressure for early marriage, immediate and continual child-bearing and, in many cases, no other alternatives perceived. The causes and consequences of these attitudes and social practices are explained below. (For a fuller description of the life of women in a Yemeni town, see Dorsky, 1981.)

Modesty: Females lag far behind their male peers in both education and employment because of customary constraints on their behaviour, having to do with modesty and the maintenance of the honourable reputation of their families. In the most extreme instances, urban females are kept in the seclusion of their-homes or fully veiled when going out for afternoon visits.

A small number of families allow their daughters to study, and a still smaller number allow them to work outside the house once they have finished studying. While numerically small, this group is increasing every year.

Age at marriage: Perhaps one of the most serious factors affecting the school dropout rate and participation in employment of young women is early marriage. The census shows that half of the Yemeni women have married by the time they are 20. A rural survey in 1977 found the singulate mean age at marriage to be 16.3 years, and in one northern village 65 percent of the females had married before menarche (Myntti, 1978a, 1978b).

Marriage in Yemen is a family, often a tribal, affair. Traditionally, groups arrange not only the participants in a wedding but the timing of it; hence, two important economic factors are considered as critical: (1) the importation of additional female labour into the extended family of the groom, and (2) the collection of a large portion of the very high bridewealth by the father of the bride. Unlike elsewhere in the Arab world, Yemeni bridegrooms are nearly as young as their brides. The brides are absorbed into the extended family, and the groom does not have to be financially or spatially independent.

Once married, a new birde has rigorous work duties in her new household, and usually begins bearing children. These activities preclude work outside the houshold for most young married women.

Traditional attitudes of husbands: In the traditional Yemeni view, the prime duty of a husband is to support his dependants (wife, female kin, parents and children). Accordingly, a wife's working for a wage reflects badly on the husband's ability to support his family, and indeed, on his performance as a husband. A woman seeks employment only if she needs the money, the reasoning goes. The visible first groups of wage-earning women appear to be the urban poor who are often migrants to the cities or of the *akhdam* social strata, and a small urban elite. The paucity of participation in this phenomenon by women in the growing urban middle class of government civil servant and merchant families, perhaps indicates that these groups are the strictest adherents of the traditional view.

Fertility and family planning: Until recently high fertility was regarded as the will of God and also a necessity. Because infant morbidity and mortality remain high, couples may fear limiting their chances for children since even their living ones might easily die. One reason why couples want several children is to assure their support in old age.

The total fertility rate in Yemen is thought to be about 6 live births per woman (Myntti, 1978a, 1978b). This is far lower than it might be, due in part to the practice of breastfeeding which prolongs the intervals between births. Breastfeeding is on the wane, however. Powdered milk can be found in the most remote villages, as can contraceptives which appear to be on the increase.

The subject of family planning is a delicate one in Yemen because strongly pro-natalist elements exist among the 'Ulama. An overt family planning campaign would only antagonize the religious authorities, but family planning services are being carried out in a discreet manner in mother and child health centers and hospitals. Contraceptives are also available in pharmacies and general stores, and are brought in by returning migrant labourers.

While it appears that more couples are dealing with the question of having children in a rational and calculated way, which ignorance surrounds the subject of contraceptive practice and women might be reluctant to use it due to frightening or negative stories heard from other women. Despite this, a 1977 survey in Sana'a by C. David and P. David found that 40 percent of the Sana'ani women preferred four or five children. About 21 percent of the women had used contraceptives and 37 percent said it would be possible in the future. Myntti found that 9 percent of rural women who had ever-married interviewed were using contraceptives. In a survey conducted by the Yemen Family Planning Association, 13.1 percent of the women were using contraceptives. Vasectomies among Yemeni men are on the increase, as the operation is reputedly easy, effective and not harmful (Myntti, 1978a, 1978b).

Lack of childcare facilities: Married women are also barred from working outside their homes because they have to care for their children. Some women are fortunate enough to have kin who can help, but few options apart from extended family support exist.

Few couples wait to have children. The pressure to have a first child soon after marriage is great, both because it improves the woman's marital security and also because it is important proof of the husband's virility. In some areas, a boy becomes a man when he has fathered his first child.

The Legal Code: The Yemeni legal system is rooted in *Shari'a*. Yemeni Muslims follow the Shafi'i, Zaydi and Isma'ili sectarian divisions which are given room for their own interpretations in the national legal system.* While many sections of the Qur'an and family law derived from *Shari'a* may be cited as discriminatory to women, Yemenis — both men and women — argue that the law is flexible and the spirit of the Qur'an is positive regarding women and work. There appear to be no laws which would discriminate against women and their work outside the home. In formal employment, women and men receive equal pay for equal work.

In summary, Yemeni women are not entering the modern, urban labour force, nor are they becoming educated as fast as they might, because attitudes exist which keep them at home to protect their modesty; early marriage and childcare do not allow them time away from home, and wage earning is considered to be a male responsibility.

*For an excellent analysis of how personal status laws actually work in a small Zaydi community see Mundy, 1979.

Policies Regarding Women and Development: The Five Year Plan 1976/77-1980/81 and 1982/83-1986/87

Perhaps the best barometer of governmental attitudes towards development is the Five Year Plan. The plan emphasizes building a foundation for development, starting with the infrastructure of the country, an infrastructure that would include such basic services as health and education.

Many government officials feel that education, for females as well as for males, is the key to the future. Education is to be wide-ranging, including formal, non-formal and applied education. A special women's section has been established in the ministry of education to improve, among other things, the health and home economics curricula for schools, and to establish adult education centers for women. School participation rates for girls are increasing, particularly in the Ibb and Ta'iz governorates. In adult literacy centers in 1981 about 30 percent (2266) of all students were female (CPO, 1982: 215).

At this stage of development in Yemen, the Government is emphasizing providing the population with services to satisfy basic needs; women are assumed to benefit from advances made in these fields. The Five Year Plan also acknowledges that women are an important source of manpower in the country: yet government officials, in their various ministerial programs, are not reflecting an awareness of how the traditional roles of women are changing. They do not seem certain of what can be done to increase female urban labour force participation, and other forms of participation. The present Five Year Plan lacks a specific program through which the maximum number of women can be put to work.

Improved Measurement of the Labour Force

Beginning in 1983, the central bureau of Statistics of the Central Planning Organization will conduct a pilot study on the problems of measuring work that is unpaid, seasonal and part-time. This study should provide suggestions on how the national statistical machinery can better measure economic activity in Yemen and will also quantify the qualitative observations on Women's work made by Myntti (1979).

Legal moves: The labour law of the government has been in effect since 1970. Those women employed in the modern sector have the right to: maternity leave with pay for a minimum of 40 days after birth, daily time off work for breastfeeding and a maximum of four months and ten days off for mourning the death of a husband. There are many examples of the Yemenis having put the principle of equal pay for equal work into practice. This holds for wage employment in the modern sector only.

One section of the revised Family Law (1978) states that every bride should have reached menarche, and that she is not permitted to leave her parental home until age 16. Early marriage will continue to be a problem in Yemen, however, and most social analyses feel that the presence of a law is unlikely to change practices.

In summary, integrating women into development in Yemen should mean: (1) letting them benefit from the extension of basic services and infrastructure; (2) acknowledging the importance of women in both the rural and urban divisions of labour; (3) concretizing the notion that female labour is important for the development of Yemen, concentrating on women as participants in development through specific programs for women in ministries, the private sector and special project components designed for women; and (4) encouraging women to gain education and training, and to participate in urban work at all levels. These points will be discussed further in the following section.

Policy Recommendations for the Integration of Women into Development
The Central Planning Organization of the Yemen Government requested a report on women and development from its West German-funded Advisory Team (Myntti, 1979). The report, published in 1979, sets forth guidelines for assuring that women participate in and benefit from the process of development.

A first step is to recognize that women play crucial roles in the household as wives and mothers, and in other productive activities. For project planners, these can be made explicit through consideration of checklists which cover the division of labour, sex ratio, age structure, traditional remunerative activities of women and so on.* Development projects should address the *real* roles that women play, improving them or adapting them to new economic realities.

One problem with government policies regarding women in Yemen is that they have been so vague that they are ignored. Following are some concrete examples of what can be done to maximize the labour of women for development.

Women in agricultural production: The ministry of agriculture should supervise the development of a broadly-based extension service, aimed at entire rural communities, and not segregated by sex or age.

Women should be trained to take advantage of the gains brought about by the mechanization of agriculture such as being taught to run machines, like threshers. More research should be conducted on appropriate agricultural technology for women in order to develop labour-saving devices for the tasks they do.

* Some examples of checklists which have been proposed: Boserup, E. and C. Liljen-crantz, 'Integration of Women in Development' (for UNDP); FAO, 'Guidelines for the Integration of Women in Agricultural and Rural Development'; IBRD, 'Integrating Women into Development', and for a summary, Van Dusen, R. (1977).

Women as housewives: After determining which elements of a traditional house should be preserved, model kitchens, lavatories and other house features could be introuced. This could be organized by the Women's Section of the Ministry of Education, or by the staff of the Yemeni Women's Association. The new ideas could be communicated through the agricultural extension system, or through the media, such as television and radio.

Education in nutrition and hygiene, childcare, and infant feeding is very necessary. With television and radio affording wide coverage, even in the countryside, they would be excellent instruement to educate women about their roles as wives and mothers.

Improvements in water systems for villages and fuel alternatives will directly benefit women. The private sector should research the market and provide the people with economical alternatives.

Women in education and the modern sector: The education system will remain of latent value until attitudes are changed. A media campaign, stressing the respectability and value of education, could stimulate the change of attitudes.

In an attempt to encourage urban women toward modern sector employment, the Women's Bureau in the Social Affairs Authority and the Yemeni Women's Association could provide information on jobs and job-related training.

Rural Yemeni Women and their Work

Work in the household

The patrilineal extended household is the ideal in Yemen, though where space and money are available, there is a definite trend to nuclear households. In the traditional household, work and social activities tend to be segregated. The senior male makes all the important decisions though the women of the household have an influence in household affairs. In most cases, women do not have overt decision-making power even if all the adult males of the household are away working, since male kin in nearby households take charge of financial and familial matters. The division of labour itself within a household is highly sex and age specific. Males go to the market and participate in public decision-making in the local mosque. Women and children manage the internal workings of the household and perform the agricultural labour.

A brief description of each activity follows. Household work in Yemen is, in some ways, more rigorous than that in other parts of the Middle East.

Water: The first Five Year Health Program (1976) states that only 8 percent of the population of Yemen has easy access to water. Improvements are being made, through local initatives but even in cities and rural towns, women who live in highland villages, built on defensible mountain pinnacles normally walk down to springs and *wadis* and return with ghee tins of water on their heads. The journey can take up to five hours.

Fetching household water is normally the responsibility of women; but sometimes children help, taking tins and donkeys to streams or wells to fetch the water. In some of the coastal villages, sweet water is brought in by truck or men carry tins balancing two across their shoulders. These services are paid for.

While chatting at village wells or public springs is pleasant for women, the work is physically strenuous and it causes many physical problems. Time would be saved and health improved if water supplies were within easier reach. Rural water supply projects are needed everywhere in the countryside to improve not only the quantity but also the quality of the water supply. Cleaner water would lessen water-borne illnesses, and increased quantities of water could make improved personal and household hygiene possible. Informal education would be needed to stimulate the awareness of problems due to poor hygiene.

Agricultural work: In the last several years Yemen has moved away from an economy dominated by subsistance level agriculture to one where agricultural work is an important activity of the resident rural population, but supplemented with cash earned by family members abroad or in Yemen's cities. Locally-produced grains are still vital to the Yemeni diet; thus women who do the bulk of work in cereal production contribute directly to their own food raising.

The work that women do within their households varies mostly by age, while the work that women do in their agricultural fields varies not only by age but by the socio-economic standing of the family and by what crops are produced in the area.

In general, old women do the lightest work in the fields. They work on their own lands or on those that their family has rented. Children help with the weeding and thinning, but the younger women do the bulk of the work.

Male roles in cereal crop production are primarily in the tasks of ploughing and threshing. Men also are responsible for all aspects of most cash crop production, *gat (catha edulis)* in particular. In areas which have been wealthy due to a long history of *qat* and coffee production, women may not do any agricultural work or participate only minimally in the cultivation of the grain crops. While grain crops account for 85 percent of the cultivation in Yemen, the mixed cropping example and its relation to women's roles is an interesting one.

In general, women of elite families do not work in agriculture to the same extent that other women do. They are restricted to their households as a sign of status as well as the moral superiority which seclusion connotes. If anything, as the cash economy permeates rural Yemeni society, the 'haves' will restrict their women and the 'have nots' will be paid to do the work. Yemen may provide an illustrative empirical example of how the working arrangements can change from the more primitive peasant model, which relies on the labour of every family member, to economic differentiation and the seclusion of the women of the elite. This trend, just beginning in Yemen, has already occurred in other Arab countries.

In the traditional division of labour for subsistence grain crop cultivation, the women prepare the soil during the winter with manure, pull out weeds and roots, sow, thin the seedlings and weed all summer, harvest in several stages, then winnow, clean and store the grain.

In some areas women are beginning to plough behind a pair of oxen, a donkey or a camel. This task and threshing are predominantly male responsibilities, as is the repairing of terraces during the winter. Out-migration of males has affected the latter task and many terraces are said to be falling into disrepair. Ploughing and threshing are, ironically, the two tasks which are easiest to mechanize in Yemen. The mechanization will help alleviate bottlenecks due to the out-migration of males at peak periods, but it will not modernize agriculture significantly nor change the tasks of women in grain production.

Work for remuneration: it is quite easy to overlook the tasks in the traditional sector for which women have earned payment. Modernization can harm these opportunities where women have to support themselves, so care should be taken to understand fully the traditional situation and possibly adapt old roles to new economic realities.

In rural towns where there is a modern sector women can work as: hospital cleaner, nurses and staff, school teachers and Qur'an tutors, bank workers, tea shop workers, or bride decorators.

In villages and rural towns women can earn money as: seamstresses water carriers, clothes washers, bread makers, basket makers, traditional health workers including midwives, construction workers, servants, traders, animal tenders, potters, weavers and agricultural labourers.

Women who are without support from men are not the only ones engaged in remunerative labour. There are women who work alongside their husbands in restaurants, construction, trading and handicrafts work.

Some of the above occupations vary by social position and region. Only rural women of the southern part of the country work in construction; they are usually paid a fraction of what men are paid for similar tasks.

Traditional healers are often of the religious elite (*sayyid*) or of the barber class (*muzayyin*) to which the decorator of the bride belongs. Tea house attendants, potters, weavers and servants tend to be of low social status.

In summary, the functioning of the subsistence agricultural economy of Yemen has always depended on the unpaid labour of women and children. With the massive out-migration of males during the 1970s, the predominantly male tasks of ploughing, threshing and terrace repair have suffered most. Mechanization with tractors and threshers may alleviate some of the bottle-necks, but it will not modernize the work of women in agriculture.

Development should be directed at rural society just as it is at city dwellers. This would include application of appropriate technological advances to the traditional tasks of women related to the household and to fetching water, providing fuel, animal care, dairy and poultry production, and, finally to agricultural work.

In general, women are not moving into new rural work roles as much as they are moving out of old ones. The growing moneyed elite now can afford to hire labour to substitute for the work of their women.

Conlcuding remarks

The extent to which women participate in formal employment in Yemen is low. This is due to many factors, including the legacy, at least until recently, of Yemen's under-development, general lack of education in the country and cultural attitudes toward women which emphasize their roles as wives and mothers. However, females now have the possibility of being educated, and, at least in the cities, the rise of modern sector work has increased the demand for all labour, including that of women.

Yemen is 90 percent rural; most of its resident population live in small remote settlements and are engaged in agriculture. Particularly in these areas, women continue to play important roles in the agricultural economy. This explicit recognition of the real work that women do is an important first step. As we have seen, the labour force participation rate tells us little about what Yemeni women actually do. Fortunately the explanatory power and applica-bility of such measures are being called into question by Yemen's main statistics-gathering agency.

What is written on women in developing countries is based on many assumptions which deserve scrutiny. For example, it is generally assumed that women should participate in wage employment. All our scales of development and modernization depend on this assumption. One wonders if this ever accurately reflects local perceptions and felt needs.

Most Yemeni women have not thought much about modern wage employ-ment. Most of them are rural, they marry, raise their children, work in the fields and their households and are reasonably content. Only a few city women have the awareness that they might be more fulfilled (to use a western phrase) if they were working for a wage outside their homes.

The perceptions of local women aside, the subject of women's work can also be viewed as part of the problem of available manpower. This is a salient development issue in Yemen, particularly exacerbated by the out-migration of working-age males to Saudi Arabia. The Yemeni government has also taken a stand, stating that women are more than half the available labour in the country and that their skills, energies and potentials should be tapped. How this is to be accomplished remains vague.

Personal constraints are always a more immediate problem than any impetus at the national level. If women are to be encouraged to participate in the development of their country through various channels of work, efforts must be made to ease their tasks as wives and mothers, for these roles are not likely to change in the near future. It is also realistic to assume that male participation in the internal affairs of the household is minimal and is likely to remain so.

Finally, one last assumption must be tackled. Implicit in much of the women and development literature, and explicit in much of the feminist literature, is the notion that the more productive the roles that women play, the more decision-making power they will have. Hence, they will have greater control over their own lives and this is beneficial. This notion is all tied up with productive roles, wages and economic independence. In Yemen, women have major productive roles but only a limited power in their households, no overt decision-making roles and no apparent control over their lives. Yet this is not a major concern with them. Their individual concerns are over less work and more cash to have a more comfortable existence for their children and themselves. This is what 'development' means to them.

The question of women and work must be seen at two levels: First, increased and improved labour participation (used in the broad sense) is beneficial at the national level. Yemen needs its womanpower at every level. Secondly, individual benefits derived from work (and easier work) are various, and in Yemen at the present time, they are not necessarily perceived as having to do with wages, compensation packages, economic independence and freedom, but with less arduous work and more cash.

Bibliography

Allman, J. and A. Hill, 1978. 'Fertility, Migration and Family Planning in the Yemen Arab Republic'. *Population Studies* 32, 1.
Birks, J., C. Sinclair and J. Socknat, 1978. International Migration Project. *Country*

58 C. Myntti

Case Study: Yemen Arab Republic, University of Durham, Department of Economics. Mimeographed.

Bornstein, A., 1974. *Food and Society in the Yemen Arab Republic.* Rome: Food and Agricultural Organization. Mimeographed.

Boserup. E. and C. Liljencrantz, 1975. *Integration of Women in Development.* New York: UNDP.

David, C. and P. David, 1977. *Preliminary Results of a Survey to Determine Women's Attitudes Toward Family Planning.* Sana'a. Mimeographed.

Dersky, S., 1981. 'Women's Lives in a North Yemeni Highlands Town'. Unpublished. Ph.D. dissertation, Case Western Reserve University.

Food and Agricultural Organization, 1977. *Guidelines for the Integration of Women in Agricultural and Rural Development Projects.* Rome: FAO. Mimeographed.

Makhlouf, C., 1979. *Changing Veils: Women and Modernization in North Yemen.* London: Croom Helm.

Mundy, M., 1979. 'Women's Inheritance of Land in Highland Yemen'. *Arabian Studies* 5: 161-187.

Myntti, C., 1978a. *The Effects of Breast-Feeding, Temporary Emigration and Contraceptive Use on the Fertility of the Yemen Arab Republic.* Cario: Programme for West Asia and North Africa. Population Council.

–, 1978b. *Women in Rural Yemen.* Report to AID, Sana'a. Mimeographed.

–, 1978. *Women and Development in Yemen.* Bonn: GTS.

Sinclair, C. and J. Socknat, 1975. *Assessment of Manpower Development and Policy and Programme Suggestions for the Yemen Arab Republic.* Sana'a. Mimeographed.

–, 1978. International Migration Project. *Migration for Employment Abroad and its Impact on Development in the Yemen Arab Republic.* University of Durham, Department of Economics. Mimeographed.

Steffen, H. and O. Blanc., 1977. *Data Bank of the Population Census.* Sana'a.

–, 1978. *Final Report of the Population Census.* Sana'a.

–, 1982. 'La Demographie de la Republique Arabe du Yemen'. In Bonnenfaut, P. (ed.), *La Peninsule Arabique d'Aujourd'hui,* Aix en Provence: Centre d'études et de Recherches sur l'Orient Arabe Contemporain.

Van Dusen, R., 1977. *Integrating Women Into National Economies: Programming considerations with Special Reference to the Near East.* Washington, D.C.: AID. Mimeographed.

World Bank, 1975. *Integrating Women into Development.*

–, 1975. *The Development of a Traditional Economy.* Yemen Arab Republic.

Yemen Arab Republic, 1970. *Legal Code, Labour Law* (In Arabic).

Youssef, N., 1974. *Women and Work in Developing Societies.* Berkeley: Population Monograph Services.

Yemen Arab Republic, Ministry of Health, 1976. *Five Year Health Programme.*

Yeman Arab Republic, Central Planning Organization, 1977a. *The Five Year Plan.*

–, 1977b. The Housing and Population Census: *Preliminary Report.*

–, 1978. *Family Law* (In Arabic).

–, 1982. *Statistical Yearbook, 1981.*

Yemen Family Planning Association, 1980. Yemen: *A General Study of Contraceptive Use.* Sana'a. Mimeographed.

Chapter 3

Women and Development in the Gulf States

H. Azzam and C. Moujabber

Introduction

The four Gulf States of Kuwait, Bahrain, Qatar and the United Arab Emirates (UAE) have been experiencing a dramatic pace in their socio-economic development over the last fifteen years, particularly since 1973. It can safely be argued that these countries will continue to be in the forefront of social and economic change for some time to come. The four countries share similar cultural, social and economic backgrounds that merit their study together as a group.

Women in this part of the world have been playing a limited role in the economically active labour force. The opportunities available for women to assume wage employment have been rather limited. Indeed, the percentage of women in the wage-earning sectors in the four Gulf countries was extremely low and it has improved only slightly in recent years. However, the reported low female participation rates do not take into account the fact that a number of women were working independently in the private sector as agricultural workers, midwives, religious instructors or in other forms of self-employment.

The process of bringing women out of seclusion started with the right to equal educational opportunities that was granted to females when the Gulf countries got their independence. In time, the women themselves became aware, through their newly-acquired schooling, that the restrictions placed upon them were more in line with traditional rather than religious obligations. They realized that women's right to gainful employment is not denied to them by the Qur'an and that in fact it has existed since the earliest days of Islam. National economic policies supported their cause, especially since rapid development and modernization continues to be the goal of the Gulf States towards which the contribution of every citizen is needed.

Contrary to the fact that in most Islamic countries women were denied their inheritance rights (Baer, 1964), women in the Gulf area have always received their willed share as designated by the Qur'an. Thus, even during the period when pearling and fishing were the primary economic activities in this part of the Arabian Peninsula, it was not unusual to find that women owned many of the ships that went to sea. Actually, some of the trading merchants were females, but they always conducted their business through men acting on their behalf, and continue to do so. Not only did women inherit money, which could be invested, but many of the ruling families' women-folk were recipients of large plots of land. After the discovery of oil, and as land began selling at a premium throughout the Gulf, some of these women became quite wealthy through the exploitation of their real estate. In contrast, opportunities remained very limited indeed for the majority of women who needed to provide an income for themselves and their children. Some raised chicken, sheep or goats and sold eggs, meat, cheese and milk from door to door. Others worked as seamstresses, healers, Qur'anic instructors and some were even employed as hair stylists. Bedouin women also sold honey as well as woollen cloth which they themselves weaved.

It was not until the discovery of oil in the region that development plans were formulated and new economic opportunities became available. The growth and prosperity experienced since, has had an impact on various aspects of the economy in these countries. Among other changes the wage earning capacity of men and women improved exceedingly. The purpose of this chapter is to present a general overview of the employment opportunities available for women in the Gulf countries today. We will then discuss the educational status of women and the effect that women's employment may have on family life in the Gulf.

Women in the Labour Force: An Overview

The transformation of potential female labour force entrant into economically active agents has been rather slow in the Gulf states, not unlike the trend in other Arab countries. By 1975, total female employment in the Gulf still represented less than 8 percent of the total labour force in the region; a proportion which would be significantly reduced if the non-national female component was excluded.

A regional picture of sectoral female labour allocation can easily be drawn for the Gulf, since the distribution of female labour among the primary, secondary and tertiary sectors of the individual countries reveals a common pattern with a predominant tertiary sector, followed by the secondary sector and lastly by the primary sector. If we are to compare this structure of employment with those prevailing in the remaining Arab countries, it would appear that the Gulf countries are the only ones in which the primary sector is a minor female labour absorber. Moreover, although the tertiary sector is also predominant in other Arab countries (e.g. Egypt, Iraq, Lebanon, Libya), the Gulf countries are the only ones which absorb practically the whole of the female work force, as is the case in Qatar (Table 1).

Female employment in the Gulf has been basically moulded by social factors since they dictate what type of economic activity is deemed appropriate. This is true in the sense that any form of female participation in the labour force needed to be in conformity with a modesty code of behaviour calling for the minimal intermingling of sexes. In this, the Gulf countries are not unique. Similar reservations prevail in most Arab countries. However, the degree of conservatism ranges from the long-standing pattern of female seclusion from economic and social life, as in Saudi Arabia, to the relatively lax attitudes of Lebanese, Tunisian and Moroccan societies. It is not surprising, therefore, that the transformation in the status of women in the Gulf was initiated by a cultural change which was soon to turn into a social change, both prerequisites for women's economic emancipation. This cycle actually began with female education becoming a reality, giving rise thereby to a demand for female teachers. In time, the need for female nurses opened up yet another remunerative employment outlet, both of which closely complied with social norms. Otherwise, household activities would have continued to be the only socially legitimate type of female activity.

It is interesting to note that even though social factors govern the allocation of female labour, the distribution of female employment by sector in the Gulf happens to be identical to the distribution of total employment, i.e. male and female. One would, therefore be tempted to say that even if these social factors were not existing, female labour allocation in the Gulf would have proceeded along the same lines, i.e. it would have favoured the tertiary sector (see Table 1). For many reasons, which we do not need to go into at this point, the tertiary sector generally has a high labour absorptive capacity. In the case of the Gulf states, however, this potential would also be reinforced as long as they maintain their commercial primacy in the Middle East. Dubai has successfully marked its place as a flourishing reexporting centre because of its strategic position and fine infrastructure facilities. In fact, it is destined to be an ideal distribution point for the whole Gulf region. Bahrain is now acknowledged as the Arab nation's banker in the market places of the world. As a financial centre, the country seems almost tailored for the role. Aside from an educated population to whom commerce has been a way of life, and its outstanding communication facilities, it is in an almost perfect location, midway between the Eastern and Western markets.

Table 1: Female employment by sector in the Gulf states and other Arab countries (Most recent years).

(percentages)

	Year	Primary	Secondary	Tertiary
Gulf States				
Bahrain	1971	0.2	4.1	95.7
Kuwait	1975	0.1	1.8	98.1
Qatar	1975	–	–	100.0
U.A.E.	1975	0.4	5.7	93.8
Other Arab				
Countries				
Egypt	1975	16.1	11.8	72.1
Iraq	1975	26.7	12.3	61.0
Jordan	1971	23.5	8.8	67.7
Lebanon	1975	21.9	22.0	56.1
Libya	1973	38.5	6.4	55.1
Saudi Arabia	1975	66.4	11.5	22.1
Syria	1975	80.9	6.8	12.3
Tunisia	1975	25.1	46.0	28.9
Yemen (A.R.)	1975	87.2	1.6	11.2
Yemen (P.D.R.)	1975	79.5	3.3	17.2

Source: Based on data derived from national censuses.

The idea that is being toyed with here is, therefore, to what extent social tradition may have resulted in sectoral mis-allocation of labour. A similar analysis as above would lead us to argue that if the primary sector in the Gulf states is but a low female labour absorber, it is probably because agricultural activities are being carried out in no more than one percent of the total land area in the Gulf. Similarly, that the potentials of the secondary sector as an absorber of labour are also low can partly be explained by the predominance of an oil sub-sector which involves highly capital-intensive activites. It should be borne in mind, however, that these countries are pursuing a policy of economic diversification with the aim of reducing dependence on oil. The employment implications are expected to be far-reaching for it has opened and continues to open a wide sphere of work opportunities both for men and women. By 1975, the UAE could boast of having had the highest proportion of the total female workforce involved in the secondary sector, followed by Bahrain (see Table 1). It is interesting to note that in Bahrain the oil company BAPCO even started running a secretarial course in which many Bahraini girls enrolled (Taki). Nevertheless, the trend of economic development is unlikely to change significantly the pattern of female employment. What it will definitely affect, however, is the level of female employment. As the region's unused human resource, potential female labour force entrants can be seen as substitutes for at least part of the expatriate labour force. The governments of the Gulf countries started becoming conscious of the increasing number of foreigners which reached alarming proportions, even in such female-stereo-typed activities as in community and personal services.

Before a successful nationalization of jobs can be secured, however, the conservative social attitudes towards female economic participation need to be neutralized. Already governments have played an active role in accelerating this process. Since 1965, the Bahraini government has been adopting an attitude of openness, such as giving young and educated people the oppor-tunity to participate in government administration and assuring female graduates of finding jobs. On the social front, many active women's associa-tions have emerged, coeducation has been introduced into many industries and the emancipation of women has made quite a headway (Taki). Less aggressive, though equally constructive, the ministry of labour and social affairs in Qatar has established a social training centre to provide training to Qatari girls and women in sewing, needlework, knitting and domestic economy. The aim of this project is to train and qualify Qataris so that they may be productive and contribute towards the development of their country (State of Qatar, Qatar Yearbook, 78-79).

It is hardly surprising that community and personal services absorb the bulk of female employment in the Gulf countries, especially that these activi-ties include medical and educational services, which together represent nearly fifty percent of total female employment in these countries. Of these two activities, however, the teaching profession appears to be the more popular employment outlet (Table 2). In Qatar, as in other Gulf countries, the absolute majority of teachers work in government schools and institutes.

Table 2: Female teaching and medical staff in the Gulf (selected years).

	Female tertiary employment	Teaching and Medical staff as a percent-age of female tertiary employment	Female teaching staff	Female medical staff
Bahrain (1971)	3072	39	994	207
Kuwait (1975)	34172	50	9760	7211
Qatar (1975)	1800	53[a]	950[b]	n.a.
U.A.E. (1975)	8950	24[c]	2128	n.a.

Source: National Popualtion Censuses.
[a] Representing public teaching staff only as a percentage of total female tertiary employ-ment.
[b] Working only in public schools and institutions.
[c] Teaching staff only.

Besides, opportunities in the medical field have yet to be fully taken advantage of. In spite of the high demand for women doctors, based on the assumption that women prefer to be treated by other women, there was only one female physician in Bahrain according to the 1971 census. Furthermore the high demand for female doctors can be reflected through the results of the Kuwaiti census which reported 114 female physicians in 1970, only 3 of whom were Kuwaitis. Female nurses, on the other hand, account for more than fifty percent of the medical corps.

The second most popular female absorbing sector in the Gulf is wholesale and retail trade, although one would expect that work in commerce would be socially unaccepted since it would expose women to strangers. Consequently, one would also expect that the position of salesgirl would be commonly occupied by non-nationals; however, such generalizations should nowadays be made with caution. Unlike the other Gulf states, finance, insurance, real estate and business services have precedence over trade as female labour absorbers in the UAE. Nevertheless, in all four Gulf countries, these two sub-sectors account for less than 10 percent of total female employment.

There has been a relatively significant increase in the share of female employment in the transport, storage and communications sub-sector. This sector's share rose from 0.3 percent of the total female labour force to 3.3 percent in Kuwait between the census years of 1970 and 1975. Since the activities that go into both transportation and storage tend to be male-oriented, it is not too presumptuous to state that the bulk of this expansion was directed towards the area of communications. Women in the Gulf have been attracted to the field of radio and television broadcasting. In fact the growth of mass media in the 1950s and 1960s contributed significantly to the emancipation of women in Bahrain (Taki). The local people's reaction to seeing women in their own country on television was not, however, entirely positive at first. Many of the older generation still consider it shameful for a woman to show her face on television and be viewed by thousands of people.

Women's interest in other fields such as law, politics, engineering and journalism is going at a much slower pace than teaching or social work, because the former are professions that require higher education and long experience. Even those women who have the necessary educational qualifications find it difficult to secure a job in these fields because many parents are opposed to their daughters entering predominantly male-controlled occupations.

Table 3 gives a clear picture of the distribution of females according to occupations in the latest census years. Clearly the majority of female workers in the Gulf are engaged in the professional or technical fields. Next comes service workers, particularly in the case of Kuwait where it represented

Table 3: Female labour force by occupation in the Gulf countries for available years.

(percentages)

Occupation		Bahrain 1965	Bahrain 1971	Kuwait 1965	Kuwait 1975	Qatar 1970	UAE 1975
Professional technical	(A)	14.3	51.6	42.2	40.6	43.2	43.4
and related workers	(B)	3.7	52.7	21.3	54.3	*	*
Administrative and	(A)	36.9[a]	2.2	2.2	0.1	2.8	0.4
managerial workers	(B)	34.2[a]	2.2	3.2	0.3	*	*
Clerical and related	(A)	*	12.3	7.2	12.2	12.3	19.8
works	(B)	*	10.2	21.8	27.4	*	*
Sales workers	(A)	2.2	1.3	0.7	0.9	1.2	1.4
	(B)	3.0	1.7	1.1	0.3	*	*
Service workers	(A)	26.2	28.7	41.8	45.3	39.3	29.1
	(B)	31.4	30.0	40.0	14.7	*	*
Agriculture, Fisher-							
men and related	(A)	0.1	0.1	0.1	–	–	0.4
workers	(B)	0.2	0.2	0.6	0.2	*	*
Production and							
related workers,							
transport equipment							
operators and	(A)	15.2	2.3	3.8	0.7	1.0	1.2
labourers	(B)	19.3	2.4	2.4	0.5	*	*
Occupations note	(A)	5.0	1.4	1.9	–	–	4.3
elsewhere specified	(B)	8.0	0.1	9.6	2.3	*	*

Source: National Population Censuses.
(A) Percentage distribution of total female employment by occupational group.
(B) Percentage distribution of *national* female employment by occupational group.
[a] Includes clerical and related workers.
– Negligible or zero.
* Not available.

upwards of 45 percent of the total in 1975. Although this major occupational group includes, among others, activities which are either malecontrolled (such as protective service workers comprising fire-fighters, policemen and detectives) or are socially rejected for national females (such as housekeeping, waitresses, cleaners and building caretakers), this high percentage is not contradictory because Kuwaiti females represented no more than 7 percent of total females in this occupation, and 14 percent of the total national female workforce. One may venture to elaborate that female Kuwaitis in this occupation are probably involved as cooks and building caretakers, i.e.

attending to the operation of an apartment house as representatives of the owner or managing agent. This conclusion is based on the fact that according to both the 1965 and 1970 population censuses, these two sub-groups together accounted for more than 95 percent of total female Kuwaiti service workers. In fact, similar proportions prevailed in Bahrain according to the population census of 1971.

With respect to the occupational trend in the Gulf, little can be said about either Qatar or the UAE. In Qatar only one census was conducted (1970) and although three censuses were carried out in the UAE (1968, 1971, 1975) detailed employment statistics can only be obtained for 1975. Of the remaining two Gulf states, Bahrain appears to have experienced the more dramatic changes in the occupational structure of its female labour force between 1965 and 1971. The phenomenal jump in the share of porfessional technical and related workers cannot be corresponded with any major changes in the remaining occupations. Undoubtedly the inflow of expatriate labour is one of the major factors underlying this change; however, data are lacking on employment by occupation, sex and nationality to substantiate this suggestion.

The effect of international migration on the occupational structure of the female labour force in the Gulf can easily be gauged from the case of Kuwait. As was previously mentioned, the occupational trend of female employment between 1965 and 1975 registers minor increases and/or decreases across occupational groups. If the expatriate female component were excluded, however, one would arrive at a completely different picture. The majority of working Kuwaiti females are no longer engaged in services, rather they are involved as professional and technical workers. The fact that the number of female service workers dropped from 40 percent in 1965 to 15 percent by 1975 can be seen as an indication that Kuwaiti women have attained a higher level of education and training than that of ten years ago. By the same token, the women who have entered the labour market in large numbers in recent years are all well qualified, enough to join professional and technical activities. In fact, the share of professional activities soared from 21 percent of the total national female workforce in 1965 to 54 percent by 1975.

Judging from the low or declining share of females in production and related jobs one can conclude that women in the Gulf are not encouraged to work in manufacturing industries. These industries depend entirely on male expatriate workers, either because there are not enough local men to fill these jobs or because nationals tend to shy away from working in manual or blue collar jobs that are often considered to be of low social status, irrespective of pay. Generally, the income incentive of the unskilled or semi-skilled manual jobs is not sufficient to attract nationals towards the socially less desirable positions.

Clerical activities in the Gulf have maintained a share of not more than

20 percent of the total female workforce. Unlike the West, such activities have not been stereotyped for women, since they involve significant inter-action between the sexes; however, degrees of variation can be found across the four Gulf states. In Bahrain, for example, secretarial jobs were open to women as early as the 1960s (Taki), whereas in Kuwait only 3 female Kuwaitis were reported as stenographers/typists by 1965.

In general, the investment opportunities for women in the private sector are quite extensive. If a woman has money or property of her own, she is free to invest it as she chooses. Many female members of wealthy families have long held title to plots of land which were acquired primarily through inherit-ance and are now being developed into modern building sites. Many women are also involved in wholesale and retail trading, such as clothing, jewelery stores, cosmetics and other business enterprises. Usually, women themselves will not appear in any front office or participate in business meetings; rather they would hire men to be their representatives for most business transactions.

Educational Status of Female Nationals of the Gulf States

In less than a decade, the illiteracy rate among women in the Gulf decreased from around 70 percent in 1969 to about 50 percent in the mid-1970s. The percentage of females with secondary school education increased from 10 percent in 1965 to around 20 percent in the late 1970s. Women with university degrees represented 0.1 percent in 1965 compared to 1 percent in 1975. The educational standard of women is expected to improve consider-ably in the foreseable future as more of them are attending schools. School attendance in the Gulf is mandatory at the primary level and is free at all school levels including university education.

Table 4 focuses specifically on the case of Kuwait, and shows that the working Kuwaiti females have attained a better standard of education at all levels since that of the mid-1960s. However, it also appears that the educa-tional drive did not take impetus except after 1970 where dramatic changes can be noticed across all levels. Primary educational attainment of Kuwaiti females increased markedly to nearly meet the proportions of non-Kuwaiti females, whereas the percentage of Kuwaitis with intermediate level schooling more than doubled to exceed that of non-Kuwaitis. Similar developments can also be distinguished both at the secondary and university levels; however the majority are still non-Kuwaitis at both levels. By 1975 only one out of every four professional women with a university degree was a Kuwaiti. Nevertheless,

Table 4: Female labour force in Kuwait by educational level and nationality, 1965-75.
(percentage)

Educational level	Nationality	1965		1970		1975	
		M	F	M	F	M	F
Illiterate or can read only	Kuwaiti	27.4	15.8	32.8	9.4	33.9	6.7
	Non-Kuwaiti	72.6	84.2	67.2	90.6	66.1	93.3
Read and write	Kuwaiti	24.2	18.1	27.7	7.4	28.8	5.9
	Non-Kuwaiti	75.8	81.9	72.3	92.6	71.2	94.1
Primary	Kuwaiti	22.1	31.3	33.9	32.5	37.7	45.2
	Non-Kuwaiti	77.9	68.7	66.1	67.5	62.3	54.8
Intermediate	Kuwaiti	20.5	22.4	28.9	26.7	35.6	58.8
	Non-Kuwaiti	79.5	77.6	71.1	73.3	64.4	41.2
Secondary and below university level	Kuwaiti	5.2	5.4	13.4	13.7	20.8	30.9
	Non-Kuwaiti	94.8	94.6	86.6	86.3	79.2	69.1
University and above	Kuwaiti	7.6	4.4	9.6	9.1	13.0	18.6
	Non-Kuwaiti	92.4	95.6	90.4	90.9	87.0	81.4

Source: Ministry of Planning, Directorate General for Planning Affairs, Labour Force Planning, The Characteristics and Trends of the Kuwaiti Labour Force, Kuwait, August 1977, Table No. 32, p. 221.

working Kuwaiti females still faired better than Kuwaiti males for whom the ratio was one to six. Except for the category of working females who can read and write only, varying degrees of this superiority existed across all educational levels.

The vertical expansion of female education in the Gulf countries was not accompanied by a horizontal diversification in the field of study that female students usually opt for. More than half of the female students at the University of Kuwait are in the school of arts and education, and out of these the majority study education, sociology and psychology. Between 1969 and 1978, female graduates from the University of Kuwait made up to 72 percent of the total in the school of arts; 54 percent in the school of science; 45 percent in the school of commerce and business administration and 39 percent in the school of law. Excepting nursing, very few go into medicine and engineering. Accounting and business administration also remain predominantly male fields of study. Female university graduates tend to gravitate to such jobs as teaching, social work and certain other office jobs that require minimal contact with the opposite sex.

Effect of Women's Employment on Family Life

The education and employment of females is expected to affect both marriage and family life, primarily in the form of delaying marriage, and perhaps reducing the number of children. In the case of the Gulf states, it is still too soon to measure these effects. All that can be said at this stage is that fertility rates remain very high. In comparison to developed economies, which have fertility rates in the order of 2.0 to 2.5, the fertility rates are certainly high in each of Bahrain (6.7), Kuwait (7.5), Qatar (7.2) and the UAE (5.9) (ECWA, 1980).

The implication of increased employment on fertility in the Gulf may be indirectly examined by the age structure of the female workforce. By 1975, the large majority of Kuwaiti women in the labour force (71 percent) were in the peak of the fertility age group, 20-29 years. This can be attributed to the fact that Kuwaiti women have only recently started to work outside the home. Though less acute in Bahrain and the UAE, with a percentage close to 50 percent, the trend of increased female labour force participation points to significant demographic changes.

The 1975 census in Kuwait shows that 39 percent of Kuwaiti female workers were single, 52 percent married, 5 percent divorced and 3 percent widowed. Meanwhile the ratio of divorcees and widows in Kuwait, as in

Qatar, to cite another example, are lower than in many other countries. These women are not compelled to work, especially as they are well provided for by the state. According to the Social Security Law of 1963 in Qatar, both widows and divorcees who have no breadwinners, whether with or without children, fall in the category of citizens who are eligible for regular monthly financial assistance of up to QR. 750 (Qatar Yearbook, 1978-79).

Conclusion

For many years the Gulf region has been one of the least developed regions of the world. However, the discovery of oil has now put the area on the crossroads of world affairs. In such a fast changing context, trying to change the centuries-old stereotyped view of women in a wife-mother role to one where they can perceive themselves in the role of students, teachers, workers or leaders is a difficult task for any society to cope with. The educational and employment opportunities now available in the four countries can help bring about this change, as similar opportunities have been the catalyst of de-stereotyping women's roles in the other Arab countries. Change will not come overnight and life will continue to be difficult for the single women but at least other career opportunities outside homemaking will be open to her. Even for married women, once their children are of school age and the use of birth control becomes widespread, they may engage in productive jobs and activites.

The fact that most working women in the countries under study are concentrated in the so-called 'feminine' occupations of education, health and social planning, should not be a cause for discouragement since these areas, like any other, are badly in need of qualified local people. As various studies have shown, women in many of these traditional occupations often have the opportunity of reaching high positions and eventually moving ahead into male-dominated professions. However, this is not to say that women should not be encouraged to enter areas traditionally dominated by men, on the contrary, it is certain that women will begin to be more involved in other professional fields. This will come true as a large number of female nationals continue to enroll in high schools and universities both in the Gulf countries and abroad, and as they start to diversify their fields of study to include, besides liberal arts and social sciences, engineering, medicince, business and sciences.

With growing manpower shortages in the Gulf, the involvement in social production of women who are still in household occupations would be of great significance. It is estimated that by 1985 the total expatriate labour force will have more than doubled in Qatar, nearly doubled in the United Arab Emirates and attained one and a half times its level in 1975 in each of Bahrain and Kuwait (Birks and Sinclair, 1979). Since women are the Gulf's unutilized human resources, better education and a more liberal stance towards female employment would render them capable of contributing to the process of growth and development in the region. As women are increasingly being encouraged to go into male-dominated fields of study, both at the university level as well as at the secondary and technical vocational levels, these countries could substitute, albeit partially, their indigenous female labour force to the increasing numbers of expatriate labour.

Undoubtedly, therefore, the situation of women in the Gulf States will improve as a result of the continual rise in the educational level, together with social and economic development. The effect of local traditions regarding sex segregation is still considerable, and no woman would embark on a career without first consulting her family, particularly the male head. With each new generation, however, more and more flexibility is expected to prevail. What is most important when one is examining the role of women in the economies of the Gulf States, whether as part of the public labour force or private investment sector, is that neither Islam nor government policy is keeping them from becoming economically active. The Islamic religion bestows economic freedom upon men and women, and the governments of these countries have been quick and wise in pointing this out. With the passing of time and especially through the effects of equal educational opportunities, it is likely that tradition will yield increasingly less weight against the forces of modernization, and women's quantitative as well as qualitative input into the economy will rise. The Gulf countries would eventually succeed in their drive to tap the much needed fifty percent of its human resources.

Bibliography

Al-Thakeb, F., 'The Kuwaiti Attitude towards Woman's Status in Our Contemporary Society'. *Studies on the Status of Women in Kuwait and the Gulf.* Kuwait. The Socio-Cultural Women's Society.

Azzam, H., 1979, *The Participation of Arab Women in the Labour Force: Development Factors and Policies.* Population and Labour Policies Programme, Working Paper No. 80, WEP, ILO, Geneva.

Baer, G., 1964. *Population and Society in the Arab East.* New York: Praeger.

Boserup, E., 1970. *Women's Role in Economic Development.* London: Allen and Urwin.
Kuwait. Ministry of Planning, Directorate General for Planning Affairs, 1977. *Education and the Labour Force in Kuwait from 1977 to 2000.* Kuwait.
—, 1977. Ministry of Planning, Directorate General for Planning Affairs. *The Characteristics and Trends of the Kuwaiti Labour Force.* Kuwait.
—, 1978. Ministry of Planning, Central Department for Statistics. *The Annual Statistics Bulletin.* Kuwait.
—, 1976. Planning Board. *Draft Five-Year Development Plan.* Kuwait.
—, 1975. Planning Board. The Special Working Team for Women's Affairs. *Document on the Status of Women in Kuwait.* Kuwait.
State of Qatar, 1978-79. Ministry of Information, *Qatar Yearbook.*
Taki, A.H., *The Changing Status of the Bahraini Women.* Bahrain: Oriental Press. n.d.
The Special Working Team for Women's Affairs, 1976. *Characteristics of the Kuwaiti Woman in the Censuses of 1957, 1965, 1970, 1975.* Kuwait.
University of Kuwait. Alumni Records Section, Registration Department, 1978. *Alumni Statistics, from 1969/1970 to 1977/1978.*
United Nations, 1975. *Status of Women and Family Planning.* New York: U.N. Publications.
United Nations Economic Commission for Western Asia, 1980. *The Population Situation in the ECWA Region,* various issues. Beirut.
Youssef, N., 1974. *Women and Work in Developing Countries.* Berkeley: California, Population Monograph Series No. 15.

Chapter 4

Labour Force Participation of Lebanese Women

M. Chamie*

At least since the 1950's, unusually large differences in family lifestyles were documented by the social scientists who have studies Lebanon (Prothro, 1974; Woodsmall, 1956; Yaukey, 1972). Woodsmall (1956 :7), for example, observed that

There is a great contrast between the swift modernization of Beirut with its concentration of material, social and cultural avantages, and the villages which lack health and educational facilities, and where the needs of young people are scarcely provided for. Even so, however, this transition has not left the village untouched. Social imbalance has been increased and the traditional fabric of rural life somewhat weakened. Those who have a deep concern for the welfare of Lebanon must discover and develop new lines of approach to rural improvement.

The contrasting lifestyles were not simply explained by rural-urban differences. The streets of Beirut in the early to mid-1970s illustrated the extent of prevalent variations in behaviour found within the swiftly modernizing city itself. One could observe women wearing traditional Bedouin or village apparel walking alongside other Lebanese women in Western fashions of all kinds. A less superficial example of contrasting lifestyles was reported in a study of Lebanese marital behaviour. Marital relationships were found to range from extremely proscribed with very little direct exchange between spouses, to very active and mutually gratifying, and from grossly inegalitarian to very equal depending substantially upon the educational status of wives (Chamie, M., 1977). The educational attainment of women in Lebanon also affected other important family characteristics. For instance, the wife's higher educational attainment was linked with declines in both desired and actual family sizes among married couples (Chamie, J., 1976).

*The author wishes to thank Ms. May Ghulmiyyah for her considerable research assistance during the preparation of this chapter. Thanks also to Dr. Richard Anker and Joseph Chamie, and Ms. Shake Sinanian and Jane Peterson for their comments on an earlier draft.

The contrasts seen in social behaviour were further magnified by the fact that the old complicated sociocultural fabric of Lebanon was rapidly unraveling while old political allegiances and economic and legislative alliances to various religious and ethnic groups remained relatively unresponsive to the change. In the midst of all this turmoil, a devastating war erupted that was highly complex in nature.

How did all this social and political upheaval affect the status and labour force participation of women? While many of the repercussions remain unknown, it is highly likely that for both women and men, the war temporarily diverted attention from their work or plans for upward mobility to the more immediate concerns for the safety and comfort of the family. Since then, population shifts in Lebanon have been at times completely unexpected and totally unpredictable. Job opportunities and daily work schedules still vary considerably depending upon the political climate and safe transportation routes throughout the country.

This rapidly changing and precarious situation, however, has actually forced women to take on new responsibilities. Women who were evacuated or displaced to villages and to abandoned city apartments took on the primary responsibility for their families' economic survival. During the war when some communities were transformed into battlefields where neighbours sometimes faced each other in combat, many men were forced to stay home for fear of their lives while women left home to find temporary work. Sewing, handwork, house-sitting for absentee owners and housecleaning became emergency occupations for women who were desperate to provide money for the family. In many respects the fighting only accelerated a phenomenon which was already occuring owing to the large out-migration of males in the early 1970s to work in other countries in Africa, the Americas and the Gulf areas. Women who remained in Lebanon took on the responsibility for managing entire families and were sometimes the heads of households for many years (Peters, 1978). The work status of women in the 1970s was also one important aspect of Lebanon's contrasting lifestyles.

The purpose of this chapter is to examine the status of working women in Lebanon during the 1970s. Labour force participation rates are presented and the occupational diversity found for men and women is compared. The chapter also examines women's comparative status within occupational sectors and compares the educational attainment of women and men who had similar occupations. Also addressed are the definitional problems of work which occur in a transitional society such as Lebanon. The realities of political and social upheaval are typical of many parts of the world and for this reason, this study of the status of women just prior to the war may prove relevant to other countries as well.

Data

Lebanon's last census was taken in 1932, therefore, no population census information about women and work is available. During the heavy fighting in 1975-76, many of the other available data bases were destroyed or left so badly damaged that repair was unfeasible. It has, therefore, become necessary to rely on the published results of two major surveys for detailed data on the status of working women.

The first survey, the *Economicaly Active Population survey of Lebanon* (EAP), was conducted in 1970 by the Ministry of Planning. The EAP survey was based upon a census of households completed by the Ministry of Planning.* It is a probability sample of approximately 30,000 households, or approximately one fifteenth of all households in Lebanon at that time. The EAP survey provided extensive information on the demographic, social, and economic characteristics of Lebanon's resident population in 1970. Its primary purpose was to describe the economically active population. Some analysis of the female labour force was completed, but the emphasis of the analysis was upon male employment.

The second survey is the 1971 *National Fertility and Family Planning Survey* (NFFP). The NFFP survey utilized the EAP survey for its sampling frame and selected a 10 percent subsample in order to study the fertility behaviour of currently married women who were between the ages of 15 and 49. Unpublished tables from Chamie's (1976) analysis were examined for relevant information about female employment. In addition to these surveys, smaller and less representative samples of the Lebanese female population were reviewed. In our discussion of levels and trends of labour force participation in Lebanon, we have referred to the 1975 ILO estimates, which are projections of the 1970 EAP survey, and other, less representative surveys not mentioned in the ILO text.

Levels and Trends of Labour Force Participation in Lebanon

The economically active population of Lebanon is defined by the EAP survey as people who hold a job for which they are remunerated with cash, or who are unpaid workers in a family enterprise from which the family is remunerated with cash, or who are searching for work, i.e. unemployed persons. Such

*For a detailed explanation of the methodology for the EAP household survey, see Ministère du Plan (1973), and Chamie, M., (1976).

a general definition excludes 'housework' and 'housewives' from the active population since such workers and jobs are erroneously assumed not to contribute to the 'cash' economy. Using this general definition, the following information is presented.

In 1970, approximately 17 percent of the labour force in Lebanon was female and 83 percent was male. In 1975, ILO estimated the proportion to be 18 and 82 percent, respectively. The annual rate of growth of the labour force between 1965 and 1970 was 2.4 percent: 0.5 percent for women and 1.9 percent for men. Since 1950 the number of women officially in the labour force has more than doubled, i.e. from 51,000 in 1950 to 112,000 in 1970 (Table 1).

Table 1: Labour force estimates and annual growth rates of the labour force according to sex for Lebanon.

	Male	Female	Total
Labour Force (In thousands)			
1950	408	51	459
1955	428	60	488
1960	452	70	522
1965	485	88	573
1970	532	112	644
1975	608	137	745
Labour Force (%)			
1950	88.9	11.1	100.0
1955	87.7	12.3	100.0
1960	86.6	13.4	100.0
1965	84.6	15.4	100.0
1970	82.6	17.4	100.0
1975	81.6	18.4	100.0
Annual rates fo growth of the labour force (%)			
1950-55	0.97	3.12	1.22
1955-60	1.08	3.26	1.36
1960-65	1.43	4.56	1.87
1965-70	1.86	5.04	2.37
1970-75	2.71	4.14	2.96

Source: ILO. 1977. *1950-2000 Labour Force.* (Geneva: ILO). Second Edition.

In 1970, women between the ages of 20 and 24 had the highest labour force participation rates, followed closely by women between 25 and 29 years old (Table 2). Participation rates for women were highest in Beirut city and in rural areas with populations less than 1,000. The rural rates were higher than the rates for Beirut suburbs and other cities, even though according to the UNESCO (1973) report, the number of women in agriculture was underestimated by the EAP survey because a considerable number of women considered farm work and housework to be closely related, and, therefore, described themselves as inactive. Age and sex differences in labour force participation are shown in Figure 1. Sex ratios of the labour force by residence status indicate that for every 3.6 men working in Beirut, there was one woman working. In rural Lebanon, there were 4.7 men for every woman in the official labour force. The ratios for Beirut and suburbs and other cities was 5.5 and 5.9 per working woman, respectively (Table 2).

Even though the above findings indicate that the growth of women in the labour force was greater than the growth rates for men, the actual participation rates are very low when compared to men. For example, whereas only 9 out of every 100 females in Lebanon were labour force participants in 1970, 43 of every 100 males were. Also, 16 percent of women between the age of 15 and 64, and 78 percent of the men in this age category participated in the labour force (Figure 1).

Composition of Female Labour Force Participation

In 1950 the majority of the male and female labour force was in the agricultural sector. By 1970, the service sector employed most working males and females (Table 3). Sector activities, however, are not so comparable for men and women. In general, women working in 1970 were in the least prestigious occupational categories of industry, service and agriculture. In addition, the spectrum of occupations within which they were employed was substantially narrower than the array of occupations performed by men.

For example, the EAP survey coded nine general occupational categories of persons working in scientific and technical professions. Whereas the distribution of men across the nine categories was diverse, 87 percent of all women were in a single occupational category — nursing and midwifery (Table 4).

In addition, among the nine coded liberal arts and humanities professions, 92 percent of the women working in this category were in one occupation, teaching. Subcategories of occupations in the liberal arts and humanities professions are shown in Table 4. These professions were called 'liberal' professions by the Ministry of Planning in Lebanon. Of the 15,510 women who taught in 1970, only a few were college professors (UNESCO, 1973). Al-Amin (1975) suggests that large numbers of women who choose teaching young children as a profession view it as a natural extension of their mother role, and, therefore, see this kind of employment as socially very acceptable.

Table 2: Age-specific activity rates of women by metropolitan status and sex ratios of labour force activity rates: Lebanon, 1970.

AGE	URBAN						RURAL	
	Beirut				Other Cities			
	City		Suburbs		1,000		1,000	
	Activity Rate[1]	Sex Ratio[2]	Activity Rate	Sex Ratio	Activity Rate	Sex Ratio	Activity Rate	Sex Ratio
0-9	0.4	25	0.1	100	0.3	100	0.3	33
10-14	10.8	55	5.1	154	5.1	120	5.8	86
15-19	17.8	201	14.9	311	9.6	342	17.8	210
20-24	33.1	200	20.6	380	20.6	319	21.3	361
25-29	28.6	311	16.1	594	17.1	540	18.4	508
30-34	24.5	395	16.4	596	11.4	831	14.1	680
35-39	15.5	634	13.8	712	9.3	1030	14.7	664
40-44	16.0	605	12.7	761	6.0	1580	14.5	663
45-49	14.7	650	11.3	814	8.9	1060	12.6	751
50-54	13.5	670	5.2	1690	5.4	1570	12.1	725
55-59	9.5	848	5.4	1390	5.5	1465	8.8	938
60-64	9.7	710	7.1	846	5.4	1220	8.8	841
65-69	4.5	1187	3.9	1090	0.7	7029	6.7	954
70+	4.5	684	1.2	1833	1.5	1720	4.5	860
Crude activity rate for women[3]	13.5		8.3		6.7		9.0	
Sex ratio of labour force activity rates (per hundred)		356		547		599		468

contd.

Table 2 (contd.)

1 Age-specific activity rate = Number of women working in each age group/total number of women in each age group X 100.
2 Sex-ratio of crude activity rates = Male activity rate/female activity rate X 100.
3 Crude activity rate = Number of women in labour force/total number of females X 100.
Source: Ministère du Plan, Direction Centrale de la Statistique. 1972. *L'enquête Par Sondaqe Sur la Population Active au Liban, Novembre 1970.* (Beirut, Lebanon: Centrale de la Statistique); Tableau 55: 109.

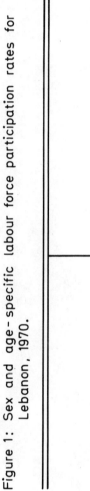

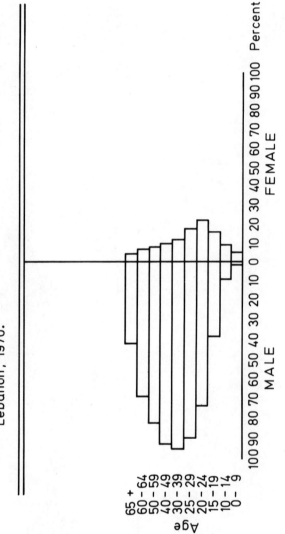

Figure 1: Sex and age-specific labour force participation rates for Lebanon, 1970.

Source: Ministère du Plan, Direction Centrale de la Statistique, 1972. L'enquête Par Sondage sur la Population Active au Liban, November 1970.
(Beirut, Lebanon: Centrale de la Statistique): Tableau 55; 109.

Table 3: Proportion of the labour force in agriculture, industry, and services by sex of worker for Lebanon, 1950-1970.

Year	Agriculture	Industry	Services
		MALES	
1950	52.60	21.80	25.60
1960	36.50	24.30	39.20
1970	18.90	26.40	54.70
		FEMALES	
1950	76.20	8.50	15.30
1960	49.90	14.25	35.85
1970	23.60	20.00	56.40
		TOTAL	
1950	55.23	20.32	24.45
1960	38.30	22.95	38.75
1970	19.72	25.29	54.99

Source: ILO. 1977. *1950-2000 Labour Force* (Geneva: ILO) 2nd Edition.

Similar patterns are repeated across all other occupations. In sum, the over-whelming majority of women who worked for remuneration in 1970 were found in the following occupations classified by category: scientific, technical and liberal arts and humanities professions (nurses, midwives and teachers of children); administration and management (managers of enterprises and secretaries); business and sales (sales clerks and commissioned sales persons); services (house servants and janitorial workers); agriculture (field labourers) and non-agricultural labourers (seamstresses). With the exception of the 225 women who reported managing enterprises, the vast majority of working women were found in low-paying and unprestigious jobs. In addition, the overwhelming majority of women were limited to certain socially-acceptable 'female' occupations.

An investigation into women who participated in Lebanon's work force in 1970 is an analysis of a very small group. If we consider all women between the ages 15-64 living in Lebanon, the proportions who worked in each occupational sector was almost imperceptible. Occupation-specific activity rates for women indicate that fewer than 3 percent were employed in the liberal arts and humanities. Occupation-specific activity rates indicate the percent of all females who are employed in any particular occupation. It was mentioned earlier in the text that for comparative purposes, 9 percent of all females and 43 percent of all males were employed in the labour force. Occupation-specific rates are simply a breakdown of the 9 percent of women

Table 4: Percentage distribution of men and women who work in scientific and liberal arts professions, the proportion of women in each occupation and occupation-specific sex ratios for Lebanon, 1970.

Scientific and liberal arts and humanities professional subcategories[1]	Men %	Women %	Proportion of women in each occupation F/F+M	Sex ratio M/F x 100
Sciences				
Physicists and chemists	3.4	1.0	8.0	1150
Architects and engineers	28.2	1.4	1.5	6333
Technicians	25.1	1.0	1.2	8450
Pilots	2.4	0.0	0.0	–
Biologists, agronomists	7.7	2.9	10.3	864
Doctors, dentists, veterinarians	23.4	6.8	8.1	1129
Nurses, midwives	8.5	86.5	75.8	32
Statistician, mathematicians	0.9	0.0	0.0	–
Economists	0.4	0.5	25.0	300
	100.0	100.0		
Total sciences	10110	3105	23.2	326
Liberal arts and humanities				
Accountants	2.6	0.0	0.0	–
Lawyers	9.7	0.2	1.3	7350
Teachers	63.0	91.8	51.9	92
Members of clergy	7.6	2.8	21.8	360
Authors, journalists, writers	5.4	0.8	9.9	911
Sculptors, painters	6.1	0.7	7.9	1162
Musicians, actors, dancers	1.9	1.7	39.6	153
Athletics, sports	1.5	0.5	21.3	367
Unclassified	2.2	1.5	33.3	200
	100.0	100.0		
Total liberal arts and humanities	22755	16905	42.6	135
Total professions	32865	20010	37.8	164

[1] Certain categories in the scientific and liberal arts professions were estimated in *'Population Active'* using supplementary sources of data, for examplem physicians, dentists and veterinarians. Small numbers in each professional category when compared to the total population of Lebanon decreased the stability of the sample estimates and led them to utilize such outside sources.
Source: UNESCO, 1973. Tableau III.3.1: 92.

who are in the labour force. Directors and managers were limited to 0.04 percent of the economically-active female population who were between the ages of 15-64. Administrative personnel and business and sales persons comprised 1.7 percent. Women in services, agriculture, and in skilled and unskilled labour outside of agriculture were each approximately 4 percent of the total female population between the ages of 15-64. It is also important to note that in all three economic sectors, no more than 3 percent of the working women were proprieters or bosses, making their numbers almost negligible. In short, women who worked in the labour force in 1970 were realtively few, and among women who worked, those holding leadership positions were rare.

Additional information that sheds light on the status of women workers in each occupational sector is their employment status (Table 5). Whereas the majority of working women were salaried employees (51 percent) and a large proportion were either working as unpaid family assistants (19 percent) or were receiving a daily wage (15 percent), men, in contrast, were less often salaried employees (35 percent) or unpaid family assistants (4.0 percent) and more often were independent workers (27 percent) or earners of daily wages (23 percent). Probably the most noteworthy distinction in employment status between the sexes is that while men tended to work more often as independent workers or proprieters (e.g. farmers and store owners), women tended to work more often as unpaid assistants in a family enterprise (agricultural labourers and store clerks in the family store). Further research is required to establish precisely the kinds of work that women do as family assistants (Kallab, 1978; Youssef, 1982). It is likely that in at least some of the cases, the husband and wife constitute a working partnership which was not acknowledged owing primarily to the way in which the survey questions were posed.

Among the various occupations in which women worked, those who worked as seamstresses and textile workers were most likely to be working independently (See Table 5). Half of the maids and women janitors and approximately one-third of textile workers and seamstresses were paid on a daily basis. The large majority of women agricultural workers (81 percent) worked as unpaid labourers for the family. Forty-three percent of women who worked as commissioned sales-persons were working for the family.

In sum, the majority of working women were salaried employees in every occupation except commerce, sales, and agriculture, where a large number of women worked as unpaid family assistants. It is likely that this is a conservative estimate of women who worked as unpaid family assistants because their work for the family was confused with their daily 'household' duties, and, therefore, went unreported.

Social Characteristics of Women Workers in Lebanon

The position of women in the Lebanese labour force is influenced by at least

Table 5: Employment status of women in selected occupations, Lebanon, 1970. (Percent distributions)

Selected Occupations	Employment status						Total	
	Independent Worker	Proprieter Boss	Salaried Employee	Paid Daily Wages	Family Assistance	Other	%	N
Scientific and liberal arts, and humanities (professional)								
Doctors, dentists, veterinarians, nurses	18.6	0.5	73.6	4.7	1.6	1.0	100.0	2895
Teachers	1.4	0.6	94.8	0.5	1.1	1.7	100.0	15510
Total professions	4.2	0.6	88.8	1.3	1.4	3.4	100.0	20010
Administration and management								
Stenographers, secretaries, keypunch operators	0.2	0.0	98.5	1.3	0.0	0.0	100.0	5985
Total adm. and management	0.3	0.0	96.8	2.2	0.8	0.0	100.0	9705
Commerces and sales								
Commissioned salesperson	6.0	0.7	44.9	5.4	43.0	0.0	100.0	2235
Total commerce and sales	25.2	1.5	37.1	4.0	22.2	0.0	100.0	3030
Services								
House help	1.3	0.0	89.2	8.3	0.4	0.9	100.0	14160
Janitorial	6.4	0.0	41.8	50.2	0.0	1.6	100.0	3735
Total services	4.1	0.9	75.4	17.2	1.4	1.1	100.0	21165

contd.

Table 5 (contd.)

Selected Occupations	Employment status						Total	
	Independent Worker	Proprieter Boss	Salaried Employee	Paid Daily Wages	Family Assistance	Other	%	N
Agriculture, forestry								
Agricultural worker	1.3	0.2	0.0	17.8	80.7	0.0	100.0	19470
Total agriculture and forestry	6.2	2.0	0.0	16.4	74.2	1.4	100.0	21240
Skilled and unskilled labour								
Textile workers	36.3	2.3	21.6	35.7	2.9	1.2	100.0	2565
Seamstress, dressmakers	46.5	3.4	16.4	28.0	4.2	1.5	100.0	12840
Total skilled/unskilled	39.0	2.8	19.5	32.6	4.7	1.4	100.0	18450
All occupations/women	11.7	1.4	51.0	14.7	19.4	1.7	100.0	94125
All occupations/men	26.7	8.9	35.0	23.5	4.0	2.0	100.0	444285
Total economically active	24.0	7.6	37.8	22.0	6.7	1.9	100.0	538410

Source: UNESCO, 1973, Tableau III, 4.2: 97-99.

three major socio-demographic variables: educational attainment, marital status and residence. We have already shown that women workers are most prevalent in Beirut and in rural areas of less than 1,000 population. We now consider the extent to which the educational attainment and marital status of women influence the likelihood that they will participate in the labour force.

The role of marriage and education upon labour force participation was examined by the Lebanese government with the assistance of UNESCO (1973). The study included women respondents from the EAP survey who were over 20 years old, and who had ever attended school; the sample size was 15,356 women, of which 2,795 had a job. It is regrettable that women who never attended school were excluded from the analysis, as this would have allowed for some very interesting comparisons especially since a large proportion of women in Lebanon (48 percent) were illiterate in 1970. No doubt, a large proportion of illiterate women are among the women who never attended school, and their particular employment problems and social characteristics would have been most interesting.

The study found that most working women were single. Among working women, 64 percent were single, 30 percent were married and 6 percent were widowed or divorced. Among women who did not work, the corresponding rates were 18, 74 and 8.

In addition to being single, working women were more educated (Figure 2). Whereas 75 percent of unemployed women in the UNESCO study had 6 or fewer years of schooling, 44 percent of employed women possessed that much education. Also, 1 percent of the educated 'inactive' and 7 percent of the educated 'active' female population were university graduates. Eight percent of educated unemployed women and 17 percent of educated employed women attended secondary school (UNESCO, 1973, p. 102).

Controls for education did not change the relationship between marital status and employment (Figure 2). At every educational level (with the exception of the university level, where widows were also very apt to be employed), single women most often participated in the labour force.

Educational attainment not only affected whether women worked, but also occupations they chose. Educational attainment and occupational status, however, were weakly correlated among Lebanese women (UNESCO, 1973). Also, educational attainment did not increase occupational diversity among women as it did for men.

What were the typical educational credentials of women who worked in a professional capacity? Women and men held comparable university degrees in the professions of architecture, engineering and medicine primarily because of the strict control these professions have over educational and certification requirements. The reader is reminded, however, that although men and

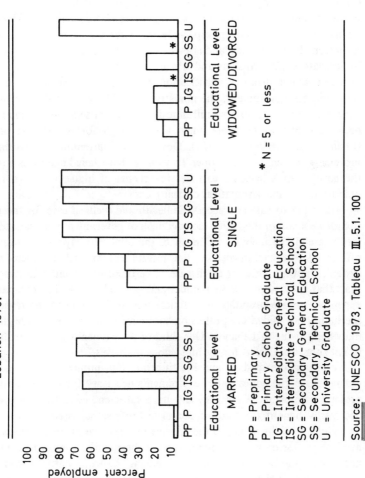

Figure 2: Percent of women over 20 years old who are employed according to educational attainment and marital status, Lebanon 1970.

Percent employed

Educational Level MARRIED

Educational Level SINGLE

Educational Level WIDOWED/DIVORCED

PP P IG IS SG SS U

* N = 5 or less

PP = Preprimary
P = Primary School Graduate
IG = Intermediate-General Education
IS = Intermediate-Technical School
SG = Secondary-General Education
SS = Secondary-Technical School
U = University Graduate

Source: UNESCO 1973, Tableau III.5.1. 100

women had the same educational training in these occupations, the actual numbers of women in the three professions were very few.

A more typical pattern of career development among professional women in Lebanon is reflected in the nursing and teaching professions, where most professional women were located. Women who worked as nurses or midwives (*sages femmes* or *dayas*), for example, generally worked in rural regions and had an elementary education or were illiterate (UNESCO, 1973; Chamie and Harfouche, 1976). Nursing, especially midwifery, is an ancient female profession in the Middle East and elsewhere; only recently has it been recognized by legislators, policymakers and the medical and health profession as an area requiring standardization, certification, training, or education. Reactions by the Lebanese government, the ministry of health, and the field of medicine have been either to ignore indigenously trained nurse-midwife practitioners, or to attempt to eradicate their jobs through formal training programs (Chamie and Harfouche, 1976). Governmental attempts to eradicate this profession, which is readily open to women, have failed mainly as a result of the government's inability to offer the clients of indigenous nurse-midwife practitioners viable alternatives of health care.

Deterrents to safe and accessible health and medical care for the population of Lebanon in the 1970s included lack of government medical and health facilities and the inability of much of the public to pay for the costly care offered almost exclusively by the private commercial Lebanese medical system. Another inhibitor to the use of certified nurses and midwives (other than that they were few in number and generally worked in comparatively expensive private hospitals and clinics) was attributable to the respect that the indigenous midwifery profession continued to have among large groups of individuals living in Lebanon. One-third of the women who delivered in 1972 in Lebanon were cared for by indigenous midwives.*

Women in the medical and health profession, primarily nurses, generally did not have the educational requirements necessary for promotion in their professional sphere. When they did have sufficient education, they did not necessarily benefit from governmental or professional assistance designed to upgrade their skills owing to the relative indifference of the government, the medical profession and the public toward their work. These effects were felt not only at the professional level influencing the work status of women, but were also felt at the personal level, affecting the health status of women and children especially. Women and infants in Lebanon received an unusually divergent range of medical assistance depending upon their access to a private physician, a medical facility, or an indigenous midwife.

---

*For further information about the indigenous midwifery profession in the Middle East, see Chamie and Harfouche (1976); El-Hamamsey (1975); and Khalil (1972).

According to the UNESCO data, teachers, unlike nurses and midwives, most typically had university training primarily in literature and social sciences. Women entering the teaching field were less educated than men and were in greater need of educational and training opportunities in order to upgrade their positions. Whereas educational attainment of most women teachers was at the intermediate level, the level for men was a university degree (UNESCO, 1973). Teaching, like nursing, lacks a strong professional association, and during the 1970s these professions offered little opportunity for advancement.

UNESCO also studied the educational attainment of women in the administrative sector who were primarily secretaries and typists. Women secretaries and typists typically had an intermediate education. Although women stenographers were more common than men stenographers, men who entered this occupation more often had special training in the area. In contrast, among machine operators (e.g. computer programmers and keypunch operators), women in this category were more highly educated than men and tended to be 'overspecialized', for example, holding a university degree, which was believed unnecessary for the job (UNESCO, 1973). Women holding university level degrees in literature, social sciences, and law found jobs with difficulty and often opted for jobs not related to their training, which resulted in overqualified, underemployed women in administration. No doubt, part of this problem is a result of the 'finishing school' mentality with which women are likely to enter universities. Many women entered Lebanese universities without receiving career counseling concerning future employment or the marketability of their skills (Al-Amin, 1975).

Although few in number, women holding degrees from technical schools at intermediate and secondary levels of education were readily hired in the area of their training, for example, practical nurses and secretaries (UNESCO, 1973). This is clearly seen to be the case in Figure 2. Before the war, there was some attempt by the government and by private organizations to increase opportunities for women in technical schools (Abu Nasr, 1978). However, only 10 percent of vocational school graduates were women (Hammoud, 1975).

In sum, professions and occupations that were readily open to women required less education and certification. Comparisons of men and women in some professions, with the exception of medicine, engineering and architecture, indicate that men in every profession were generally more educated than women and, therefore, had greater opportunity for promotion and salary increases.

Women who worked, regardless of their educational attainment, were confined to a limited number of occupations. The educational attainment of women in these fields was also low and opportunities for further training after beginning the profession were few. Among professions typically taken up by women, such as nursing, midwifery and teaching, there were few incentives offered by the Lebanese government and professional associations for stricter certification and further specialization. Requirements for entering these fields were largely undefined, or disregarded. Certification procedures were weak, if they existed at all. In the spring of 1978, an urgent bill was forwarded to the Lebanese Parliament and passed (Decree number 1077) which placed formal educational requirements and restrictions on the nursing profession. This law is still in the process of being implemented.

Although the larger trends would lead one to be optimistic about the employment status of women in Lebanon, such as increased rates of labour force participation, larger numbers of women working in a professional capacity, greater numbers who worked in the industrial and service sector rather than agriculture, these findings in themselves are misleading. More careful analysis of these data shows that women were generally poorly educated. They were typically ocnfined to positions without authority or power. Their work was restricted primarily to a few socially acceptable occupations. Although a large proportion of women working in the labour force earned monthly wages, a significantly larger proportion of women than men were working as family assistants in agriculture and in commerce, etc. and were not paid regular wages for their work. University training did not increase occupational diversity for women.

Married Women Who Worked

Marriage had a strong negative association with female labour force participation. Approximately 9 percent of the married women of reproductive age who were interviewed in the NFFP survey had an occupation other than houseworker (Chamie, 1976). However, 22 percent of all married women in the survey reported that they worked before marriage. The most significant difference between married men and women was the clear cut difference in their reported occupations. As work is currently defined, married men were members of the labour force, and married women were generally not. There was no probe in the NFFP survey to ascertain the kind of work the 93 percent of married women who reported 'housewifery' as their occupation were actually doing.

The NFFP survey did offer information on how religion was associated with wife's educational attainment, her work status, family income and fertility behaviour (Chamie, J., 1977). The data presented in Table 6 show that non-Catholic Christian women were the most educated, and had a mean of 5.2 years of schooling. Druze and Catholic women had 4.5 and 4.4 mean years, respectively, Sunni women had 3.3 years and Shi'a women average 1.6

Table 6: Educational and income characteristics of married women between the ages of 15-49 and their husbands, according to the couples' religious affiliation, Lebanon, 1971.

Background Characteristics	Religious Status					
	Christian		Muslim			
	Catholic	Non-Catholic	Sunni	Shi'a	Druze	Total
Wife's Education Mean number of years attended school	4.4	5.2	3.3	1.6	4.5	3.6
% never attended school	29	20	49	70	23	40
Husband's education Mean number of years attended school	5.4	5.8	4.5	3.3	5.1	4.9
% never attended school	15	13	29	31	10	21
Family income Average family income (LL)[1]	7173	7112	5571	4532	6180	6247
% earning less than 1500 LL per year	6	8	15	22	11	12
Total	925	592	564	567	119	2767
n.a.						28
Total sample						2795

[1] U.S. $1.00 = 3.00 LL.
Source: Chamie, 1976: Table 6.7, p. 142.

years. Over 70 percent of Shi'a women never attended school as compared to 49 percent of Sunni women, 29 percent of Catholic women, 23 percent of Druze women, and 20 percent of non-Catholic Christian women. Educational attainment, therefore, was very different for women of different religious sects. A similar association between education and religion is found for husbands. However, as might be expected, husbands were more educated than wives in every religious sect.

Family incomes also differed by religious status. Catholic and non-Catholic

Christian families earned substantially more than did Sunni, Shi'a or Druze families. Among the Muslim sects, Druze families had the highest incomes, followed by Sunni, then Shi'a families. In 1970, approximately 22 percent of Shi'a families earned less than 1000 LL (US$450 at that time) annually, compared to 6 and 8 percent of Catholics and non-Catholic Christians, respectively. As mentioned in the introduction, such socio-economic diversity was apparent during the 1970s.

Given the current definition of work used by the government, Druze and Catholic wives had most often worked both before and after marriage although their numbers were small, 9.2 and 8.1 percent, respectively (Table 7). Among women who had ever been labour force participants, there were similar proportions of Catholics, non-Catholic Christians and Druze (29, 30 and 25 percent, respectively). Sunni and Shi'a women had the least amount of work experience (17 and 16 percent, respectively).

One of the most significant factors affecting work status of married Lebanese women is work experience before marriage. Table 7 shows that for all five major religious groups, women who worked before marriage had the highest probability of working after marriage. Among Sunni women who had worked six or more years before marriage, almost 50 percent continued to work after marriage. Similar trends were found for the other religious sects although the proportions who worked after marriage were lower.

The data in Table 8 show that for married Lebanese women of reproductive age in general, there was a substantial and positive assocaition between age at marriage and work experience before marriage. An examination at the bivariate level indicates that 8 percent of the women who had married between the ages of 12 and 16, and 42 percent of women who married after the age of 25 were labour force participants. It is not clear whether women who delayed marriage did so because of work, or whether not marrying encouraged women to work.

The educational attainment of both husbands and wives was positively associated with work experience prior to marriage for women, although the association was stronger with wife's educational attainment (Table 8).

Except for families who earned more than 15,000 LL per year (which had lower proportions of women who worked before marriage than did families who earned between 10,000 and 14,999 LL), family income was also positively associated with wife's work experience before marriage. It is likely, given the social and cultural patterns in Lebanon at that time, that a larger proportion of husbands with incomes over 15,000 LL married women without work experience mainly because marriage was still likely to be contracted between families. Under these circumstances, wealthier men were unlikely to meet their future wives at work.

However, almost half of the men who were in a professional or technical

Table 7: Proportion of married women between the ages of 15-49 who worked before and after marriage by religious status, Lebanon, 1970.

| Wife's work status | Religious Affiliation | | | | | |
| | Christian | | Muslim | | | |
	Catholic %	Non-Catholic %	Sunni %	Shi'as %%%	Druze %	Total %
Worked *before* and *after* marriage	8.1	6.9	5.7	3.2	9.2	6.4
Worked *before* marriage only	19.7	20.2	9.4	10.8	12.6	15.6
Worked *after* marriage only	2.1	3.2	2.3	2.5	3.4	2.5
Never worked	70.2	69.7	82.6	83.5	74.8	75.5
	100.0	100.0	100.0	100.0	100.0	100.0
Proportion who *ever* worked	29.8	30.3	17.4	16.5	25.2	24.5
Proportion who ever worked						
After marriage	10.1	10.2	8.0	5.7	12.6	8.9
Before marriage	27.7	27.1	15.1	14.0	21.8	21.9
Total	916	590	563	564	119	2752

Source: National Fertility and Family Planning Survey for Lebanon, 1971.

occupation married women who had worked before marriage. The association between husband's professional occupation and wife's work experience before marriage is strong for Catholic and non-Catholic Christians, less strong among Shi'a Muslims and least strong among Sunni Muslims (Table 8).

Wife's labour force participation before marriage was also associated with family residence. For example, wives residing in places with a population of more than 10,000 had the most work experience before marriage.

Finally, recently married women (those married between 1960 and 1970) were more apt to have worked before marriage than women married before 1960 (Table 8). This finding suggests that work experience prior to marriage might have been increasing among Lebanese women.

How do these associations hold up when studying wife's labour force

Table 8: Percent of married women between the ages of 15-49 who worked before marriage according to the couples' selected background characteristics, Lebanon, 1971.

| Background characteristic | Religious affiliation | | | | | |
| | Christian | | Muslim | | | |
	Catholic %	Non-Catholic %	Sunni %	Shi'a %	Druze %	Total %
Age at marriage (wife)						
12-16 years old	7.1	12.3	7.3	6.8	11.1	8.0
17-19	17.9	17.8	10.0	13.9	15.0	15.0
20-21	22.6	22.0	21.6	16.0	14.3	20.6
22-24	43.4	35.0	22.9	18.9	43.8	34.3
25-40	49.1	43.9	33.3	23.0	46.7	41.6
Marital duration						
0-4 years	42.3	44.2	28.3	26.2	32.0	36.2
5-9	35.1	33.0	17.0	16.2	25.0	26.3
10-14	29.9	26.3	16.5	13.7	20.8	22.8
15-19	24.8	22.8	11.6	7.2	21.7	17.9
20+	12.6	16.2	5.7	10.1	11.1	11.4
Wife's years attended school						
0	21.5	11.5	10.7	11.8	17.9	14.0
1-5	20.9	17.5	11.3	13.8	17.6	17.1
6	23.5	29.8	18.2	16.7	15.4	23.7
7-11	41.1	39.8	29.5	25.0	63.6	38.7
12+	60.0	56.1	33.3	53.3	18.8	50.2
Husband's years attended school						
0	22.9	14.3	12.4	9.8	41.7	15.1
1-5	23.4	22.4	11.0	13.4	13.1	18.1
6	27.0	23.3	25.0	15.1	20.0	23.5
7-11	30.4	32.4	23.9	21.4	23.5	28.3
12+	42.9	45.7	19.3	30.6	42.9	37.8
Total family income (LL)						
Less than 3,000	21.6	17.1	14.7	13.3	21.0	16.8
3,000-5,999	24.3	27.5	14.4	14.4	26.3	20.7
6,000-9,999	27.6	28.4	12.5	20.4	11.8	24.1
10,000-14,999	46.8	50.0	25.8	11.8	33.3	40.8
15,000+	35.8	40.4	27.3	26.1	22.2	34.0
Husband's occupation						
Professional/technical	51.9	60.0	15.8	33.3	*	48.3
Business/management	26.6	25.8	15.7	10.8	17.4	21.3
Clerical	34.2	34.2	25.4	17.9	15.4	28.9
Police/army/guard	17.3	25.9	19.2	16.7	12.5	18.6
Craftsman	29.1	28.6	13.2	18.1	29.0	23.9
Farmer	16.7	13.6	00.0	8.5	0.0	10.9
Peddler	0.0	*	22.2	9.1	*	17.0
Labourer	26.3	19.6	14.3	13.6	21.7	18.4
Other	34.0	18.4	8.9	13.8	*	21.2

contd.

Table 8 (contd.)

Background characteristic	Religious affiliation					
	Christian		Muslim			
	Catholic %	Non-Catholic %	Sunni %	Shi'a %	Druze %	Total %
Size of place of residence						
more than 10,000	35.0	32.9	17.5	17.1	27.3	25.6
1,000-10,000	21.8	22.7	5.0	5.6	18.2	18.3
less than 1,000	21.9	9.5	1.4	14.6	17.0	15.0
Total	916	590	563	564	119	2752
n.a.						43
Total Sample						2795

Source: Same source as in Table 7.

participation *after* marriage? Although substantially weaker, the above relationships remained after marriage. Wife's age at marriage, her educational attainment, her husband's educational status, and family income were all positively associated with her participation in the labour force after marriage. The proportions who worked, however, were substantially lower at each level. For example, whereas 50 percent of married women with 12 years or more of schooling worked before marriage, 30 percent worked after marriage. Also, whereas 48 percent of women married to men employed in a professional or technical field worked before marriage, 26 percent worked after marriage.

At the bivariate level, there was a negative association between work experience and the family sizes of married women who were between the ages of 15 and 49. For example, whereas women who did not work after marriage had a mean number of 4.5 children ever born, women who worked after marriage had an average of 3.4 children (Chamie, 1976). A similar negative association was found between wife's work before marriage and the mean number of children ever born. However, even though the direction of the results were the same, none of the variance was explained by these two variables in a multivariate analysis (multiple classification analysis) done by Chamie (1976) which predicted the mean number of children ever born to Lebanese women of reproductive age. The net effects of wife's work experience before and after marriage were negligible (Table 9). There were also no strong multiple correaltions found between the predictor variables on wife's work experience and the mean number of children ever born for the five major religious sects, i.e. Catholic, non-Catholic Christians, Druze, Sunni and Shi'a Muslims (Chamie, 1976). The association, therefore, between the experience of working in the currently defined labour force and women's family sizes appears to be very week, if there is any association at all.

Table 9: The mean number of children ever born for married women between the ages of 15-49 according to the couples' background characteristics, Lebanon NFFP 1971 survey (Multiple classification analysis).

Background characteristics	Grand mean	Group mean	Gross effect	Net effect	Total N
Total sample	4.37				
Age at marriage					
12-16 years old		5.35	0.98	0.20	575
17-19		4.76	0.40	0.22	786
20-21		4.03	-0.34	-0.07	480
22-24		3.82	-0.55	-0.12	461
25-40		3.23	-1.14	-0.46	425
Marital duration					
0-4 years		1.08	-3.28	-2.87	445
5-9		2.95	-1.42	-1.29	520
10-14		4.42	5.47	0.09	639
15-19		5.73	1.36	1.23	448
20+		6.59	2.22	1.91	700
Wife: number of years attended school					
0		5.75	1.39	0.69	1077
1-5		4.24	-0.13	-0.22	759
6		3.29	-1.08	-0.50	393
7-11		2.67	-1.70	-0.79	282
12+		2.30	-2.07	-0.66	241
Size of place of residence					
Over 10,000		4.12	-0.24	-0.51	1603
1,000-10,000		4.52	0.15	0.05	630
Less than 1,000		4.94	0.57	0.09	519
Husband: number of years of schooling					
0		5.62	1.25	1.40	564
1-5		4.83	0.46	0.11	1165
6		3.43	-0.94	-0.37	344
7-11		3.33	-1.03	-0.06	251
12+		2.77	-1.60	-0.12	405
Total family income (LL3,00-US$1.00)					
Less than 3,000		5.00	0.63	0.01	939
3,000-5,999		4.38	0.02	0.06	754
6,000-9,999		3.91	-0.45	-0.03	336
10,000-14,999		2.97	-0.01	-0.28	184
15,000+		3.25	-0.01	-0.22	212
Husband's occupation					
Professional/technical		2.45	-1.92	-0.37	120
Business/management		3.93	-0.43	-0.17	460
Clerical		3.34	-1.03	-0.02	336
Police/army/guard		3.98	-0.39	0.05	172
Craftsman		4.27	-0.10	-0.04	557

contd.

Table 9 (contd.)

Background Characteristics	Grand mean	Group mean	Gross effect	Net effect	Total N
Farmer		5.50	1.13	0.14	238
Peddler		6.26	1.89	1.05	47
Labourer		5.11	0.74	0.08	592
Other		4.33	-0.04	0.13	160
Wife worked *before* marriage					
Worked		3.25	-1.11	-0.03	604
Did not work		4.68	0.31	0.01	2148
Wife worked *after* marriage					
Worked		3.37	-0.99	-0.07	245
Did not work		4.46	0.10	0.01	2507
Total					2572
n.a.					43
Total Sample					2795

Source: NFFP Survey and Chamie, 1976.

Understanding Women's Work

No doubt, one of the more significant barriers to improving the status of women's work in countries such as Lebanon is the poorly delineated definition of work used by policymakers, governmental agenices and social scientists, which leads to serious misconceptions about who is economically productive and who is not. Such assumptions not only lead to poorly conceived or inadequate policies, but also affect research conclusions.

For example, it is likely that the lack of clarity in the explanation of how women's work influences fertility is largely attributable to social scientisits', especially economists', underlying assumptions about work. Stycos (1976) concluded that informal support systems for women who work are very different depending upon social class and culture. These differences could have a substantial influence upon fertility. Rural women in Lebanon who carry their children to the fields do not have the same childcare problems as do urban working women who are required to leave their children at home and to travel long distances to work. A country such as Lebanon, for example, has few 'babysitters' compared to the United States because the concept is largely inappropriate to a Middle Eastern society. Most family networks ensure almost continual access to childcare because children are readily shifted to the care of mothers, mothers-in-law, and siblings. In the higher socio-economic classes, childcare is supported readily by assistance from servants in addition to the assistance offered by relatives. Childcare shared among family members is less common in Western countries such as the United States; even when it is available, it is generally not encouraged. These and numerous other cultural differences need to be included in any model for the study of the effects of labour force participation upon completed family size.

Social norms encouraging strong family ties, obligatory respect for older parents, and parental trust of other family members (such as grandparents) to care for children may be significant facilitators to improving women's work status while, at the same time, supporting large families. This is because such norms disperse 'motherhood' responsibilities onto a number of individuals instead of relying solely upon one person for childcare. Particular cultural patterns, simply because they are traditional need not necessarily be barriers to women working outside of the home. Neither must work always inhibit fertility. Far greater care needs to be taken to assess the social conditions which are barriers to working women and which are facilitators.

The planned facilitators for improving the status of women such as legislation and policy development, while they do exist in Lebanon, have not always been implemented. For example, although we found legislation guarding the rights of women in Lebanon, the extent to which women are aware that they have these rights remains to be seen. The degree to which legislation for women is followed up in the courts is also questionable. In addition, certain kinds of legislation actually place barriers in women's paths, for example, the strong statements in the Lebanese Family Code about the power of authority of husbands over wives' occupations, or the exclusion of married women from nomination to diplomatic and consular corps.

Legislation is also complicated by the fact that the religious law is legally binding on certain women's issues, just as is civil law. This results in policies for women being piecemeal and fragmented owing to separate court procedures for each religious sect. Attempts to draft civil legislation that counteracts religious laws are not readily supported owing to the fact that the various religious leaders are reluctant to relinquish their authority over the people in their own sects.

Social researchers and policymakers who are concerned with women and labour force participation must develop more sensitive social indicators and measures of work. In many respects, researchers who study female employment have yet to address the most crucial questions: 'What is work', and 'Who is a labour force participant?' Why is it assumed, for example, that household workers in transitional societies such as Lebanon are not labour force participants? A more realistic perspective would encourage researchers and policymakers to view household workers as members of the fourth occupational sector − 'The Household Sector' − which is the unacknowledged sector in labour force participation. Household workers, or those persons who work primarily in their homes and who produce crucial goods and services for the country, are not properly acknowledged in labour force research and policy. The assumption that these workers are a productive part of the economy would in itself change the image and status of millions of women. Their unacknowledged work would then be open to legislation on such factors as social security, work benefits, sick leave, health care, fair wages, opportunities for further specialization, etc. Currently, the majority of women who work are outside of the boundaries of work legislation.

Within the proposed household sector, numerous subcategories of employment are relevant. Household workers who produce and store foods, who care for domestic animals, who make clothing, who collect fuel for heat and cooking, or who are responsible for the care of elderly and indigent persons are to be differentiated from houseworkers who prepare already produced foods, who primarily entertain, or who are home receptionists. Certain houseworkers are essentially administrative and managerial in their orientation while others are undoubtedly unemployed, underemployed, seasonal workers, retired, or are employed in more than one capacity. These variations in household occupations and specializations need to be assessed.

In addition to this larger question of who participates in the labour force, there is the important task of identifying women agricultural workers and those who work as family assistants. As already mentioned, the most difficult problem is that these persons themselves may not consider their work to be economically important. Owing to the way in which work in the home is currently viewed by most societies, women often consider it to be 'non-work' or peripheral to the economic well-being of the family. Women who help their fathers, brothers, and husbands in the fields are apt to see this work as an extension of their housework rather than as agricultural work. When asked whether they work or not, women respond 'no' because they subscribe to definitions of work similar to the ones currently used by most policymakers. They might as well have been asked, 'Are you a man?'

Questions and probes used in census and surveys need to be posed very carefully in order to ensure their validity and reliability in identifying family assistance workers. Culturally and linguistically appropriate questions that improve our understanding of women workers must be designed. For example, during a survey of labour force participation in Syria, Syrian men were initially asked whether their wives worked. A large proportion said they did not. However, when asked, 'If your wife did not assist you in your work, would you be forced to hire a replacement for her?', the answer was an overwhelming 'yes'. Similar sensitivities to the way in which questions about women's work were constructed were found by Anker and Knowles (1978) in Kenya. They noted that estimates of the adult female activity rate in their Kenya study varied from about 20 percent when the word 'job' was used to about 90 percent when the word 'work' was used. Such findings suggest caution in wording and greater care in using the appropriate colloquial expressions for work prior to instituting larger-scale surveys from statistical offices to measure labour force participation.

Our findings for Lebanon point to the need for careful reassessment of how women should be and are integrated into the existing labour force. It is not sufficient, for example, to limit governmental policies to such a broad objective as increased participation of women. The characteristics of women who work, the quality of work that women do, the kinds of opportunities open to women who work for further specialization and promotion, the degree of respect and concern demonstrated by governments and professional associations for upgrading occupations, and the extent of diversification and career development offered to women are key factors in any assessment of their status.

Findings from surveys conducted during the 1970s in Lebanon indicate the need for explaining why women, even highly educated women, are generally confined to lower echelon positions in the formally accepted definition of the workforce and to a limited number of occupations. Statistical analyses of women and work must proceed beyond looking at broad social trends to more thorough and multivariate analyses of such factors as occupational diversity, status within occupational sectors, educational attainment of workers within occupations, sex-ratios in occupations, comparative income, and the role of part-time employment in the economic development of women.

In addition, it must be determined why the occupational sector which is most readily open to women, the household sector, remains unacknowledged as an important part of the nation's workforce. For some years now the idea that household workers are a productive part of the eocnomy has been discussed (Anker, 1982; Boserup, 1971; Jelin, 1982; and Tabbarah, 1977). Actually acknowledging this fact, however, by including household workers as members of the workforce would require a significant change in attitude on the part of economists, other social scientists and policymakers. An even more puzzling assumption, that household workers in Middle Eastern societies are virtually identical in status, income generation, power, prestige, productivity, and specialization, needs to be challenged. Obvious examples of occupational variations in household work are demonstrated by observing women who reside and work in the households of prime ministers, members of parliament, large farm owners family business entrepreneurs or tobacco labourers. The requirements of household workers, and numbers of hours worked, are substantitally different in each of these family household status categories. The support systems for their household work would vary considerably, e.g. with respect to childcare, economic returns, community involvement, seasonal demands, work hours, and work space. Such distinctions call for improved methodology when styding household work so that the occupational and employment status of household workers is accurately measured.

It would, therefore, seem to be the case that factors influencing the status of working women in Lebanon are derived from both conceptual inadequacies in the definitions of work as well as from structural influences affecting work opportunities for women. Policies and plans for improving the status of women may attain greater relevance and effectiveness as some of these conceptual and methodological problems are clarified.

Bibliography

Abu-Nasr, J., 1979. 'Women's Employment in Lebanon'. *Al-Raida*, 2, 9.

Al-Amin, R., 1975. *Al Mara'a Wal Watha'ef fil Qita'ain 'e 'am Wal Khass*. (Women and Jobs in the Public and Private Sectors). The Seventh Conference for the Committee of the Rights of Lebanese Women, March 6-7, Beirut: UNESCO.

Al-Raida, 1978. 'Article 562 of the Lebanese Penal Code Must Be Amended', 4, 10.

Anker, R., Buvinic, M. and Youssef, N.H. (eds.), 1982. *Women's Roles and Population Trends in the Third World*. London: Croom Helm.

Anker, R. and Knowles, J.C., 1978. 'A Micro Analysis of Female Labour Force Participation in Africa'. In Standing, G. and Sheehan, G. (eds.), *Labour Force Participation in Low-Income Countries*. Geneva: ILO. Mentioned in Anker 1982.

Barakat, H., 1979. *Lebanon in Strife: Student Preludes to the Civil War*. Austin: University of Texas Press.

Boserup, E., 1971. *Women's Role in Economic Development*. London: George Allen and Unwin Ltd. 2nd Ed.

Bureau of Lebanese and Arab Documentation, 1968. *Code of Labour, ARGUS of Lebanese Documents*. Beirut. Translated by Bustros, G.M. London.

Chamie, J., 1976. *Religious Fertility Differentials in Lebanon*. Ph.D. Dissertation, Sociology. Michigan: University of Michigan, Ann Arbor.

—, 1976-77. 'The Lebanese Civil War: An Investigation Into Causes'. *World Affairs*, 139, 3, 171-188.

—, 1981. *Religion and Fertility: Arab Christian-Muslim Differentials*. London: Cambridge University Press.

Chamie, M. and Harfouche, J.K., 1976. *Indigenous Midwives in Lebanon*. Occasional Monograph Series 8. *The Organization of Family Planning Programs: India, China, Costa Rica, Venezuela, Lebanon*. Washington, D.C.: Interdisciplinary Communications Program, Smithsonian Institution, 183-223.

Chamie, M., 1977. 'Sexuality and Birth Control Decisions Among Lebanese Couples'. *Signs: Journal of Women in Culture and Society*, 3, 1, 294-312.

Deeb, G., 1979. *Wajibat al Walidain Nahou el Tifl*. (Parents' Obligations Towards their

Child). Breast Feeding Workshop. Beirut: Lebanon Family Planning Association. The American University of Beirut (In Arabic).

Dibs, T., 1975. *Al-Mara'a wal Mihan al Hurra.* (Women and Liberal Professions). The Seventh Conference for the Committee of the Rights of Lebanese Women. March 6-7. Beirut: UNESCO (In Arabic).

El-Hamamsy, L., 1975. *The Data of Egypt-Survival in a Modernizing Society.* Unpublished paper from the Social Research Center, The American University in Cairo 45.

Haddad, W., 1978. 'The Legal Provisions Governing the Status of Women in Some Arab Countries'. *Population Bulletin,* UN/ECWA 14, 26-46. Beirut.

Hammoud, R., 1976. 'Naseeb al Inath fi Nitham al Ta'aleem fi Lubnan'. (Women in the Lebanese Educational System). *Majallat al Abhath al Tarbawiya,* 1, 33-57. Beirut, School of Education, The Lebanese University (In Arabic).

Jelin, E., 1982. 'Women and the Urban Labour Market'. In Anker, R., Buvenic, M. and Youssef, N. (eds.), *Women's Roles and Population Trends in the Third World.* London: Croon Helm.

Kallab, I., 1975. *Al-Mara'a fil Hirmil.* (The Women in El-Hirmil). A lecture presented in a panel discussion held at Beirut University College, May 7. Beirut: Institute for Women's Studies in the Arab World, Beirut University College (In Arabic).

Khalil, F.A., 1972. 'Indigenous Midwifery in Selected Villages in the Second Governorate of Peoples' Democratic Republic of Yemen'. M.A. Thesis Sociology. Beirut: American University of Beirut.

Ministère du Plan, Direction Centrale de la Statistique, 1972. *L'enquête par Sondage sur la Population Active au Liban.* Novembre 1970. Beyrouth: Centrale de la Statistique.

Peters, L.E., 1978. 'The Status of Women in Four Middle East Communities'. In Beck, L. and Keddie, N. (eds.), *Women in the Muslim World.* Cambridge, Massachussetts: Harvard University Press.

Prothro, E.T. and Diab, L.N., 1974. *Changing Family Patterns in the Arab East.* Beirut: The American University of Beirut.

Salibi, K.S., 1976. *Crossroads to Civil War: Lebanon 1958-1976.* New York: Caravan Books.

Stycos, J.M. and Robert, H.W., 1967. 'Female Working Roles and Fertility'. *Demograph 4,* 210-217.

Tabbarah, R., 1977. 'Population and Development in Lebanon'. *Population Bulletin.* UN/ECWA 12, 12-19. Beirut.

–, 1979. 'Background to the Lebanese Conflict'. *International Journal of Comparative Sociology* 20, 1-2, 102-121.

UNESCO, 1973. *Etude sur les Relations Existant Entre l'Education et les Possibilites d'Emploi Offertes aux Femmes au Liban.* Beirut: UNESCO.

United States Department of Labor: Bureau of Labor Statistics, 1966. *Labour Law and Practice in Lebanon.* BLS Report 304: U.S. Government Printing Office.

Woodsmall, R.F. and Charlotte, J., 1956. *The Role of Women in Lebanon, Egypt, Iraq, Jordan and Syria.* The International Federation of Business and Professional Women. Woodstock, Vermont: Elm Tree Press.

–, 1979. 'Background to the Lebanese Conflict'. *International Journal of Comparative Sociology* 20, 1-2, 102-121.

Yaukey, David., 1972. *Fertility Differences in a Modernizing Country: A Survey of Lebanese Couples.* Princeton: Princeton University Press.

Youssef, N.H., 'The Interrelationship Between the Division of Labour in the Household, Women's Roles and Their Impact on Fertility'. In Anker, R.; Buvinic, M. and Youssef, N. (eds.), *Women's Roles and Population Trends in the Third World.* London: Croom Helm.

Chapter 5

Female Labour Force Participation in Jordan

G.B.S. Mujahid*

Introduction

Jordan, like most other countries of the Middle East, is characterised by low female labour participation rates. The crude female participation rate — defined as the percentage of economically active in total female population — is only about 4 percent. Only 8.4 percent of females of working ages (15-65) are reported as economically active, constituting a mere 10.5 percent of the country's total workforce. Apparently there exists considerable scope of increasing the participation of Jordanian women in economic activity. Higher levels of female participation would help in reducing the currently high dependancy burden and contribute towards raising household living standards. At the same time, by ensuring the provision of appropriate vocational and technical training to the increasing female workforce, the country could seek to overcome certain skill shortages it has been increasingly faced with, particularly as a result of migration of workers to the oil-rich Gulf states.

*This chapter is a revised version of a working paper produced when the author was assigned as an I.L.O. Expert to the Department of Human Resources, National Planning Council in Amman under the project: Comprehensive Population and Manpower Planning funded by the UNFPA. The author is indebted for comments on the earlier version to Dr. Ghazi Farooq (ILO, Geneva), Dr. A-Majeed Khan (Education Advisor to the President of Bangladesh and formerly UNFPA Regional Coordinator), Mr. Q.U. Khan (Joint Director, Institute of Applied Manpower Research, New Delhi and formerly ILO Expert in Amman), Dr. Nabil Khoury (ILO, Beirut) and Dr. Yaser Sara (Director, Department of Human Resources, National Planning Council, Amman).

Conceptual Problems

The most important conceptual problem concerns the appropriate measure of labour force participation. The labour force participation rate is conventionally measured as the ratio of economically active — that is, employed plus unemployed — to population. The time-duration of employment can also be taken into consideration whereby the labour input is then quantified in terms of hours, weeks or months. The concept can be further refined to take account of the period for which an individual considers himself available for and is prepared to work. Limitations of data preclude the use of these refined concepts and leave no alternative to following the basic conventional approach in the case of Jordan.

The second conceptual problem is concerned with the definition of working-age population. While persons of all ages are found to be economically active to some extent, the analysis of activity rates is confined here to those who are 15 years and more but less than 65. The importance of the under-15 and over-65 in the labour force of Jordan has been declining. Of the male labour force in 1961, 2.8 and 3.7 percent respectively were below-15 and over-65.* By 1976, these percentages had fallen to 1.3 and 2.7 respectively.** Similarly, of the female labour force in 1961, 7.3 percent were under-15 and 1.3 percent over-65. By 1976, these figures had dropped sharply to 1.6 and 0.4 respectively. An increasing proportion of Jordan's labour force has thus been drawn from those aged 15-65 years. In 1961, 93.7 percent of the total labour force was between ages 15 and 65. In 1976, this proportion had risen to 96.2 percent. With further economic development, the importance in the labour force of the under-15 and over-65 can be expected to dwindle further. This is likely to be more so in the case of the under-15 whose participation in future could be ruled out if laws pertaining to compulsory education upto age 15 are strictly enforced.

Participation Rates in Jordan

The main sources of information on various characteristics of the population and labour force in Jordan are the Population Census of 1961 and the Multipurpose Household Surveys of 1972, 1974 and 1976. The Agricultural Census

*(All figures for 1961 in this section have been obtained from *First Census of Population and Housing, 1961*).
**(All figures for 1976 in this section have been obtained from *The Multi-purpose Household Survey, 1976*).

and the Labour Force (non-agricultural) Census carried out in 1975 provide the latest available count of the labour force. The National Fertility Survey of 1972 and the Jordan Fertility Survey of 1976 provide information on a number of socio-economic characteristics of a sample of ever-married women. This study draws on all these sources of information.

The age and sex-specific labour force participation rates from the 1961 Census and the 1976 Survey are summarised in Table 1. The figures show that female participation rates are highest for the age-group 20-24, and decline gradually for older ages. It is also evident that the participation rate of

Table 1: Labour force participation rates in Jordan, 1961-1976.

| | Labour force as percentage of population | | | |
| | Females | | Males | |
Age-group	1961	1976	1961	1976
15-19	3.9	3.6	57.0	29.3
20-24	5.5	22.6	90.0	80.2
25-29	3.4	18.1	94.0	96.4
30-39	2.6	6.5	92.3	97.6
40-49	2.3	3.0	92.5	93.3
50-59	1.6	1.6	83.0	82.7
60-64	1.0	1.1	69.1	55.0
15-64	3.3	8.4	83.2	73.3
All ages	2.2	4.1	50.9	33.3

Sources: *First Census of Population and Housing, 1961* (Department of Statistics, Government of Jordan, 1964), Vol. 2, and *The Multi-Purpose Household Survey, 1976* (Department of Statistics, Government of Jordan, 1977).

females of working ages went up by more than 5 percentage points between 1961 and 1976. While the participation rate of females in the age-group 15-19 declined slightly, there was a spectacular increase in the participation rate of females aged 20-29 years, and a moderate increase in that of females in other age-groups. The decline can be attributed to increased enrolment in educational institutions which also explains the observed decline in the participation rate of males aged 15-19 and 20-24. Data on enrolment from the same sources show that the percentage of females in age-group 15-19 attending schools went up from 10.9 percent in 1961 to 66.7 percent in 1976. Enrolment ratios of males went up during the same period from 30.5 to 71.9 percent for those aged 15-18 and from 4.4 to 23.8 percent for those aged 19-24. However, the participation rates of females continue to be far below international levels. This is clearly brought out by a comparison of three macro measures of female participation for Jordan and nine other countries with comparable per capita incomes (Table 2).

Table 2: Indicators of female labour force participation in selected countries.[a]

| Country | Female labour force[b] as percentage of | | |
	Total female population	Females aged 15-64	Total labour force
Dominican Rep. (1979)	17.9	27.1[c]	26.0
Ecuador (1974)	9.3	17.7	17.1
Guatemala (1979)	7.9	8.2	14.0
Jamaica (1978) [d]	38.3	68.8	47.4
Malaysia (1976)[d]	26.0	43.1[c]	35.0
South Korea (1975)	28.9	49.2	38.6
Syria (1979)	7.0	14.0	14.9
Tunisia (1979)	11.1	19.2[c]	18.9
Turkey (1975)	25.6	46.3	35.4
Jordan (1976)	4.0	8.4	10.5

[a] With per capita income (1977) U.S.$900-1,200 as listed in *World Development Report, 1980* (The World Bank, August 1980).
[b] Defined as the economically active aged 15-64, except for Jamaica (14-64).
[c] Females aged 15 and more.
[d] Peninsular Malaysia.
Sources: *Yearbook of Labour Statistics* (I.L.O., Geneva) various issues. For Jordan: *The Multi-purpose Household Survey, 1976.*

Labour Force Estimates

An analysis of the industrial and occupational structure of the female labour force is essential to a study of the overall participation rates. The industrial distribution of the labour force for 1961 and 1976 is given in Table 3. The very low proportion of agricultural labour force shown by the Household Survey 1976 suggests considerable under-enumeration in the agricultural sector. This is confirmed, as discussed below, by the labour force count for this sector made under the Agricultural Census of 1975.

Estimates of the labour force by three broad categories — agriculture, non-agriculture and unspecified — are given in Table 4. The figures for the agricultural labour force have been obtained from the Agricultural Census and those for non-agricultural workers from the Labour Force Census of 1975. Both the Population Census of 1961 and the Household Survey of 1976 include a category of 'unspecified activities' which perhaps also cover defence

Table 3: Industrial structure of the labour force, 1961 and 1976.

Industrial sector	Percentage of labour force[a]			
	Male		Female	
	1961	1976	1961	1976
Agriculture, hunting, forestry and fishing	34.6	6.3	4.7	1.1
Mining and quarrying	2.3	0.9	c	0.2
Manufacturing	7.0	10.5	35.6	10.2
Electricity, gas and water	0.4	1.1	0.1	0.1
Construction	10.6	10.6	0.3	0.6
Commerce	8.2	19.6	2.9	3.8
Transport, storage and communications	3.6	10.2	1.0	4.3
Services[b]	33.4	40.8	55.4	79.7
Total	100.0	100.0	100.0	100.0

[a] Includes workers of all ages.
[b] Includes activities not adquately described.
[c] Negligible.

Sources: *First Census of Population and Housing, 1961*, Vol. 2; and *The Multi-purpose Household Survey, 1976*.

personnel. An estimate of the numbers in this category for 1975 has therefore been added to ensure comparability.

The most striking feature of the estimates presented in Table 4 is that these indicate a higher level of female participation than that obtained under the Household Survey. While according to the Survey 10.5 percent of the total labour force consisted of females, data presented in Table 4 indicate that females comprise 16.9 percent of the labour force. This necessarily implies also that the crude participation rate of females shown by the Survey as 4.1 percent would be higher by roughly 60 percent (It must be pointed out here that this includes workers of all ages while the figures in Table 2 above cover workers aged 15-65 only). Though these higher rates do not alter the basic premise of this study that female participation rates in Jordan continue to be considerably low, it would be in order to seek a plausible explanation for the discrepancy in the two sources of information.

Table 4: Labour force by sex and sector, 1975.

	Males	Females	Total
Agriculture	84,028 (24.2)	41,014 (11.8)	125,042 (36.0)
Non-agriculture	110,458 (31.8)	17,774 (5.1)	128,232 (36.9)
Unspecified*	94,397 (27.1)	– (–)	94,397 (27.1)
Total	288,883 (83.1)	58,788 (16.9)	347,671 (100)

*Estimated.
Figures in parentheses are percentage of total.
Sources: *General Results of the Agricultural Census, 1975* (The Hashemite Kingdom of
Jordan, Department of Statistics, 1977); and *The Labour Force Census, 1975*
(The Hashemite Kingdom of Jordan, Department of Statistics, 1975).

The distribution of the agricultural labour force by employment status as
derived from the Agricultural Census is given in Table 5. The most important
category is that of 'permanent paid workers' inasmuch as these cannot

Table 5: Percentage distribution of agricultural workers by sex and employment status, 1975.

	Male			Female		
	Paid	Unpaid	Total	Paid	Unpaid	Total
Permanent workers	10.6	45.3	55.9	2.6	61.5	64.1
Temporary workers	8.1	4.0	12.1	2.8	9.8	12.6
Occasional workers	26.6	5.4	32.0	14.8	8.5	23.3
All workers	45.3	54.7	100.0	20.2	79.8	100.0

Source: *General results of the Agricultural Census, 1975.*

'avoid' being counted as agricultural workers. In addition, 'permanent unpaid'
male workers would also report themselves as working in the agricultural
sector. However, most of the temporary and occasional male workers,
whether paid or unpaid, are more likely to report their non-agricultural
activity – work outside agriculture being considered generally more 'prestigious'. Among females, most of the temporary and occasional workers, both
paid and unpaid, as well as most of the permanent unpaid workers would, due
to cultural factors, prefer not to report any economic activity (the influence
of cultural forces on female participation will be discussed in a subsequent
section). The distribution of agricultural workers by employment status
reported in the Household Survey shows that this may have actually happened
to quite an extent.

Among male workers reported in the agricultural sector in the Survey, only 57.0 percent reported themselves as being 'own account' and 'family workers', whereas the Census showed 89.4 percent of male workers as unpaid or non-permanent. Among the female agricultural workers enumerated in the Survey only one was listed under 'own account workers' and none as 'family workers' (it should be pointed out, however, that only 17 female agricultural workers were enumerated under the Survey). The Census, however, counted 79.8 percent of all female agricultural workers as 'unpaid' and another 17.6 percent as paid but non-permanent. Serious under-reporting of unpaid and non-permanent agricultural workers, especially of females, is therefore evident in the Household Survey.

Industrial Structure of Female Labour Force

In the light of the above review of labour force estimates for 1975, it would be appropriate to treat the agricultural and non-agricultural labour force separately. From Table 4 above, it is clear that if all types of workers in agriculture were to be taken into account, almost 70 percent of the total female labour force would be classified in that sector. Moreover, women would constitute 33 percent of all agricultural workers. However, if the agricultural labour force were to be defined to include only paid and permanent female workers and all permanent male workers, then females would constitute only 2.2 percent of the agricultural labour force. Also, only 5.7 percent of the female labour force could then be considered as being employed in agriculture. On the basis of information given in Tables 4 and 5, and this definition of agricultural labour force, there were 46,972 male and 1,066 female agricultural workers. The inclusion of temporary and occasional workers, specially those categorised as unpaid or family help, thus increases the extent of female participation.

Differences in the treatment of agricultural workers in various sources of information has rendered data available incomparable. Luckily, this problem does not arise in the case of the non-agricultural labour force. The distribution of female non-agricultural workers by industrial sectors as also the proportion of females in each sector's total labour force (Table 6) bring out the following salient features of the non-agricultural female labour force:
(1) More than three-fourths of female non-agricultural workers have been employed in the services sector. The manufacturing sector has been the second most popular choice of these workers. Taken together, the two

Table 6: Industrial structure of the non-agricultural female labour force.

	Percentage of labour force			Percentage of females in sectoral labour force		
	1961	1975	1976	1961	1975	1976
Mining and quarrying	neg.	0.7	0.2	neg.	0.6	2.3
Manufacturing	37.4	20.3	10.3	16.3	18.8	10.0
Electricity, gas and water	0.1	0.2	0.1	1.0	1.5	0.6
Construction	0.3	0.1	0.6	0.1	0.2	0.7
Commerce	3.0	2.4	3.8	1.3	1.8	2.2
Transport, storage and communications	1.0	2.7	4.3	1.0	3.4	4.6
Services (includes unspecified)	58.1	74.3	80.6	6.0	23.8	18.2
Total	100.0	100.0	100.0	5.3	13.9	11.8

neg. = negligible.
Sources: *First Census of Population and Housing, 1961,* Vol. 2; *The Labour Force Census, 1975;* and *The Multi-purpose Household Survey, 1976.*

sectors have employed over 90 percent of the female labour force out-side agriculture.

(2) Barring the mining sector and electricity, gas and water services (which are the least significant in terms of employment size), construction has absorbed the lowest percentage of the female work force. This is explained by the heavy manual labour which construction work mostly entails.

(3) Commerce and transport sectors, in spite of increasing their share of female workers, still employ less than 5 percent of the non-agricultural female labour force.

(4) The sectoral preferences of female workers are also reflected in the pro-portion of females in the labour force is found to have been highest in the services and manufacturing sectors and lowest in construction.

(5) The changes which took place in the industrial structure between 1961 and 1976 indicate a growing tendency on the part of female workers to enter the services sector. The proportion of the female labour force employed in the services sector jumped from 55 percent in 1961 to 80 percent in 1976. On the other hand, preference for the manufacturing sector has been on the decline but the sector still remains the second largest employer of non-agricultural female workers.

Occupational Structure of Female Labour Force

The distribution of female workers by occupational categories excluding 'agricultural and related workers' (Category 6 under the International Standard Classification of Occupations) given in Table 7 shows that considerable changes took place in the occupational structure of the female non-agricultural work force during the period 1961-1976.

Table 7: Occupational structure of the non-agricultural female labour force.[a]

	Percentage of labour force			Percentage of females in occupational group		
	1961	1975	1976	1961	1975	1976
Professional, technical and related workers	28.7	57.0	57.7	28.1	35.7	41.4
Administrative and managerial workers	0.1	0.9	0.8	0.4	3.8	3.5
Clerical and related workers	6.9	11.4	19.4	5.0	15.1	19.5
Sales workers	1.0	1.2	2.4	0.5	1.1	1.7
Sub-total white collar workers	36.7	70.5	80.3	8.2	19.6	20.1
Production and related workers, transport equipment operators and labourers	40.3	20.6	11.3	3.8	7.6	3.2
Service workers	23.0	9.0	8.4	11.2	10.5	9.7
Total	100.0	100.0	100.0	5.3	13.9	11.8

[a] For 1961 and 1976, members of the armed forces are included in every occupational group to which they belong. Figures for 1975 exclude the armed forces.
Sources: *First Census of Population and Housing, 1961,* Vol. 2; *The Labour Force Census, 1975;* and *The Multi-purpose Household Survey, 1976.*

In 1961 the highest proportion of the non-agricultural female labour force was categorised as 'production and related workers, transport equipment operators and labourers'. Thus the largest single category of female workers constituting 40.3 percent of the female labour force outside agriculture could be described as 'blue collar workers'. Next came the category of 'professional, technical and related workers' which alone accounted for 28.7 percent and, together with other 'white collar workers' for 36.7 percent of the female labour force. Then came workers in 'services' comprising 23 percent of all female workers. However, taking total labour force within each occupational category, the proportion of females was highest among professionals and second highest among workers in services. Of all 'white collar workers' 8.2 percent were females whereas in the total non-agricultural labour force females were only 5.3 percent.

By the year 1976 the occupational pattern had changed dramatically. The proportion of 'blue collar workers' and 'service workers' in the female labour force declined — the former from 40.3 to 11.3 percent and the latter from 23.0 to 8.4 percent. As against this, the proportion of 'white collar workers' went up from 36.7 to 80.3 percent, within which the category of professionals doubled its share of female workers from 28.7 to 57.7 percent. This increase in the proportion of 'white collar workers', though part of an overall trend observed also for the male labour force (see Jordan, 1981) was much more marked among female workers. This is brought out by the increasing representation of females in the higher occupational categories. While in 1961, 28.1 percent of the country's professionals were females, in 1976 they constituted 41.4 percent of this group. Similarly, the proportion of females increased sharply among clerical workers from 5.0 to 19.5 percent, and among 'administrative and managerial workers' from 0.4 to 3.5 percent. Of all 'white collar workers' 8.2 percent were females in 1961, and 20.1 percent in 1976.

It must be pointed out that one explanation of why some of the figures for 1975 fall out of line may be the exclusion of the armed forces. As we can assume armed forces to be comprised predominantly (or even wholly) of males, the occupational structure of the female labour force remains unaffected by their inclusion or exclusion. However, the exclusion of the armed forces would have the effect of increasing the proportion of females in the total labour force and hence the 13.9 percent shown for 1975 is on the high side. It would also tend to result in a higher figure for the proportion of females in groups which would include members of the armed forces, the effect being larger where the concentration of the armed forces is greater. The effect is, therefore, likely to be most pronounced among 'blue collar workers' and this explains the high figure of 7.6 percent shown for 1975. The 'white collar workers' excluding 'sales workers' are also likely to be similarly affected.

Evidence from the three sources on the occupational structure of the labour force shows conclusively that among female non-agricultural workers, 'white-collar workers' have increased at a much higher than average rate, and now constitute an overwhelmingly large proportion of the female work force. The representation of females has also been greater in the higher occupational categories. On the whole, the female labour force has become increasingly more 'top heavy' than the male labour force. These results are compatible with the increasing proportion of female workers going into services sector which includes public administration, business and financial services as well as health and education. Moreover, these changes in both the industrial and occupational structures suggest that much of the increase in overall female participation rates observed over the period 1961-1976 came from increasing participation of the educated.

Factors Influencing Female Participation Rates

The level of education is just one of several factors which are known to influence female participation rates in developing countries. A number of studies (see country studies in Standing and Sheehan, 1979) have led to the identification of the following as the important determinants of female labour force participation: cultural values, marital status, level of education, fertility, husband's occupation, household or husband's income, degree of urbanisation, and migrant status. Unfortunately, lack of data precludes analysing the role each of these factors has played in influencing female labour force participation in Jordan. An attempt is, therefore, made to discuss the influence of as many of these factors as availability of data permits.

Cultural Factors

Cultural factors are known to play a significant role in determining female labour force participation rates. In some cultures, for example, there is a stigma attached to women taking up a paid job. In Jordan, as in all other Muslim countries, traditionalism based on Islamic values has been the strongest cultural force. It is known to adversely influence female participation mainly through the institution of *purdah* which advocates segregation of the sexes and, in its extreme form, leads to a virtual seclusion of women from social life barring them from any outdoor activity. The adverse effect of such a system on participation of women in economic activity is self-explanatory.

The striking difference between female labour force participation rates in Muslim and non-Muslim countries (Table 8) reflects this cultural influence. Muslim countries are here defined as those in which the proportion of Muslims in the population is 75 percent or more. In such countries, the percentage of economically active females among females of working ages is less than half of that in non-Muslim countries. Moreover, the participation rates are even lower in the Arab countries. This could be explained by two factors. First, the proportion of Muslims in the population of most Arab countries is over 95 percent – in many, nearly 100 percent (in Libya, Saudi Arabia and all Gulf countries). Second, unlike the non-Arab Muslims of Bangladesh, Indonesia and Pakistan, the Arabs have remained free for a much longer period from the influences arising out of living together with sizeable non-Muslim populations.

Table 8: Female labour force participation in Muslim and non-Muslim countries, 1975.

	Labour force as percentage of population in age-group	Percentage of females in labour force[a]
	15-64	
All countries	46.8	35.0
Developed	53.7	39.7
Less developed	43.4	32.8
Non-Muslim	50.1	36.6
Muslim[b]	23.4	21.3
(Non-Arab)	(28.7)	(24.8)
(Arab)	(8.0)	(8.8)

[a] Defined as the economically active population in age-groups 15-64.
[b] With at least 75 percent Muslim population.
Source: Calculated from information for 119 non-Muslim and 28 Muslim (including 15 Arab) countries given in *Yearbook of Labour Statistics, 1978* (I.L.O., Geneva).

The influence of present-day Islamic values on female participation is also reflected in the occupational preferences of female workers. The most significant aspect in this respect appears to be the very low preference of females in Muslim countries for becoming 'sales workers' – an occupation in which the likelihood of indiscriminate contact with outsiders is highest. The wide differences that exist between Muslim and non-Muslim countries in respect of women's preferences for becoming 'sales workers' are brought out by evidence from ten Muslim and ten non-Muslim countries with comparable per capita incomes selected on the basis of data availability (Table 9). This shows that the proportion of females in 'sales workers' is much lower in the Muslim countries – the only notable exception being Indonesia.

While the above inter-country comparison puts the relationship between present-day Islamic values and female economic activity in proper perspective, the argument would be further strengthened if similar differences could be shown to exist in participation rates of Muslim and non-Muslim females within the same country. Unfortunately, information on differences in economic activity by religion is not easily available for most countries.

Table 9: Female preferences for sales occupations in selected Muslim and non-Muslim countries.

		Percentage of females in sales workers	Female sales workers as a percentage of female non-agricultural labour force
Muslim countries			
Bangladesh	(1974)	1.2	4.3
Egypt	(1978)	4.5	4.1
Indonesia	(1976)	48.3	40.9
Iran	(1976)	1.4	0.8
Jordan	(1975)	1.1	1.2
Libya	(1973)	0.6	0.7
Pakistan	(1980)	2.2	5.3
Syria	(1979)	1.3	1.7
Tunisia	(1975)	3.5	1.1
U.A.E.	(1975)	0.8	1.4
Non-Muslim countries			
Dominican Rep.	(1970)	20.2	5.5
Ecuador	(1974)	27.1	14.2
Ghana	(1970)	70.7	52.2
Guatemala	(1979)	34.8	16.5
India	(1971)	6.6	21.2
Jamaica	(1976)	63.3	20.0
Korea	(1975)	43.4	24.4
Malawi	(1977)	19.8	17.1
Philippines	(1977)	60.7	25.5
Thailand	(1978)	59.9	40.6

Sources: *Yearbook of Labour Statistics* (I.L.O., Geneva), various issues. For Jordan: *The Labour Force Census, 1975.*

Evidence has, however, been available for Bangladesh and Pakistan. In both countries participation rates of Muslim women have been much lower than those of non-Muslim women. (Pakistan, 1963). In Jordan, for example, some evidence can be derived only from the Fertility Survey of 1976. This indicates lower participation among Muslim women: 9.4 percent of ever-married Muslim women were reported as 'currently working' as against 16.8 percent of ever-married non-Muslim women. Moreover, 77.5 percent of the Muslim women and only 59.1 percent of the non-Muslim women were reported as having 'never-worked'.*

*(*Jordan Fertility Survey, 1976*) is also a survey of 189 women working in five institutions in the private and public sector and showed that 32 percent were non-Muslim which far exceeds the national average of about 8 percent in total population (see Jaber, Ati, and Gharaibeh, 1977). It must be pointed out that Islam does not provide the only example of cultural obstacles to female participation in the labour force. Among high-caste Hindus, for example, the taking up of employment by women is considered shameful (see Anker, and Knowles, 1979).

Marital Status

Marital status is known to cast a significant influence on female labour force participation. Information on participation rates of Jordanian women according to marital status (Table 10) shows these to have been highest for single women and lowest for married women in most age-groups. The overall pattern of the relationship between participation and marital status in Jordan is not difficult to explain and is thus similar to that found in many other countries (see for example, studies on Colombia by Angulo and Rodriguez; Mexico and Costa Rica by Uthoff and Gonzalez; Nigeria by Standing and Sheehan; and Yugoslavia by Rasevic in Standing and Sheehan, G. (eds.), 1979), difficult to explain. Married women are more likely to be burdened with family responsibilities as well as have means of financial support. This makes it both necessary and possible for them to remain out of the labour force. The opposite is true of single women, for whom the likelihood of

Table 10: Female labour force participation by age and marital status, 1976.

Age	Single	Married	Widowed	Divorced
15-19	3.9	0.8	*	*
20-24	42.2	3.6	0.0	28.6
25-29	58.8	6.4	5.9	39.3
30-34	43.8	4.7	15.9	29.4
35-39	30.8	2.6	11.3	29.4
40-44	21.9	2.1	9.6	13.3
45-49	20.7	1.1	5.8	*
50-54	11.5	0.5	4.4	*
55-59	8.0	0.9	2.4	*
60-64	8.8	0.4	1.2	*
15-64	18.6	3.1	–	–
20-44	45.1	4.0	10.4	29.6

*Less than 15 cases reported.
Source: *The Multi-purpose Household Survey, 1976.*

having household responsibilities and other means of financial support is much less. Employers also have a preference for single women having no family responsibilities, so that it may be easier for the unmarried to find a job. This factor is, however, unlikely to be crucial in Jordan or in any other country facing manpower shortages. The divorced and widowed fall in between these two categories – the former having generally higher participation rates than the latter. This may be because, given the socio-cultural set-up in Jordan, financial support from family sources is likely to be more readily forthcoming for the widowed.

Evidence from the Jordan Fertility Survey of 1976 too reveals a higher participation rate of 21.2 percent for women not living with their husbands as against a rate of 9.3 percent for those 'currently married'.

Level of Education

The level of education attained is found to exert a considerable positive influence on women's participation in the labour force. In many countries it has been found that the more highly educated females have a higher rate of participation in economic activity (see, e.g. Farooq, 1972; Pecht, 1979). For Jordan, it is known that both the overall participation of females in the labour force and the incidence of education among women have gone up since 1961. *Prima facie,* therefore, one can say that for Jordanian women, too, education and participation would be positively correlated.

Two sets of female participation rates by educational status derived from the Household Survey of 1976 and from the Fertility Survey of 1976 (Table 11) reveal a similar pattern: (1) on the whole participation rates and level of education are positively correlated; (2) participation rates rise significantly among women who have completed secondary education; and, (3) participation rates are highest for females who have received vocational and technical education.

Evidence on the relationship between level of education and work status provided by the National Fertility Survey conducted in 1972 (Table 12) supports the above findings. We use the term 'work status' instead of 'participation rate' because it is not possible to separate out women who could be described as 'currently working'. Nevertheless, the figures show the same pattern — for each stage at which work has been reported, the incidence of employment rises with education. Moreover, the figures fall in line with those of the Fertility Survey of 1976 in that the participation rate first declines with primary education and then rises with the level of education. This pattern is also common in other developing countries (Standing, 1976). Why females with less than secondary education have lower participation rates than those who have had no schooling may be because they are not prepared to do unskilled jobs while at the same time they are not sufficiently qualified for better types of jobs.

The positive relationship between education and female participation rates may ultimately be explained by socio-economic factors. Education loosens the grip of orthodox cultural values. Indeed, the very fact that they have attended schools indicates that the educated females come from less orthodox

Table 11: Female labour force participation and level of education in Jordan, 1976.

Level of education	Labour force as a percentage of population[a]	Level of education	Percentage of ever-married women[b] currently working	never worked
Less than elementary	0.7	No schooling	8.6	78.0
Less than preparatory	2.9	Primary	4.1	85.1
Less than secondary	5.1	Preparatory	7.0	80.7
Tawjihi or matric	45.9	Secondary	31.6	38.5
Post-secondary diploma	83.3	Institute	78.6	8.4
University	84.0	University	51.8	15.9

[a] 12-64 years.
[b] Sample of 3612 ever-married women.
Sources: *The Multi-purpose Household Survey, 1976* and *Jordan Fertility Survey, 1976.*

Table 12: Working status by educational attainment, 1972.

Educational category	Percentage of females[a] in each category who			
	Worked before marriage	Worked after marriage	Worked before and after marriage	Never worked
Illiterate	11.3	3.7	9.2	72.3
Preparatory and primary	9.0	2.6	4.2	82.5
Secondary and vocational	18.7	5.6	18.4	56.6
University and higher institutes	25.0	5.8	48.1	21.1

[a] Covers 5,214 ever-married women. Row totals do not add to 100 due to non-responses.
Source: *National Fertility Survey in Jordan, 1972* (Government of Jordan, Department of Statistics, 1976).

families. Moreover the greater the number of years for which a family allows a girl to receive formal education, the less orthodox is it likely to be. Similarly, the higher the level of education a girl has attained, the greater are her chances of marrying a more highly educated man having more liberal views with respect to the participation of females in economic activity.

There are also underlying economic reasons which could explain the positive relationship between education and female participation. Since a cost is incurred in obtaining education, one of the key determinants of a girl going in for higher levels of education would be her intentions of taking up a paid job. Also, as a more educated girl has greater chances of getting a better paid job, the 'opportunity cost' of a girl remaining out of the labour force increases with her level of education. Moreover with the higher pay it becomes easier to afford employing a domestic servant for taking care of or assisting in household work. It has also been observed, that the number of children a woman has is inversely related to her level of educational attainment (Table 13). This may also be a factor contributing to the positive relationship between level of education and rate of labour force participation.

Table 13: Fertility and level of education among females in Jordan, 1972 and 1976.

Level of education	Age of mother (years)				All ages
	Less than 25	25-34	35-44[a]	45 and over[b]	
	(average number of children ever-born)				
1972					
Illiterate	2.0	5.6	8.0	8.6	6.0
Primary/preparatory	1.7	4.8	6.5	7.3	4.0
Secondary	1.4	3.3	4.3	4.7	2.7
University	1.2	2.3	*	*	2.3
1976					
No schooling	2.2	5.5	8.3	9.1	6.3
Primary	1.8	4.9	6.3	7.7	3.7
Preparatory	1.5	4.1	4.9	6.3	3.0
Secondary	1.0	3.0	4.3	5.1	2.9
Institute	1.1	2.5	3.8	*	2.4
University	*	1.9	3.2	*	2.0

*Less than 5 cases reported.
[a] For 1972: 35-39.
[b] For 1972: 40-49.
Sources: *National Fertility Survey in Jordan 1972;* and *Jordan Fertility Survey, 1976.*

Fertility and Family Size

The influence of fertility and the associated responsibilities of bringing up children on female participation rates has received considerable attention in the literature (for references, see Standing, 1978). As responsibilities of motherhood and the pressure of household work demand much of a woman's time, higher levels of fertility and larger families are found to be associated with lower rates of female economic activity. This is found to have been the case in both developed and developing countries (see, for example, Cain, 1966; Cohen, 1969; Elizaga, 1974; and Pecht, 1979). We have already seen how household responsibilities are reflected in participation rates of married women being considerably lower than those of single women (see Table 10, above). In this section, we shall examine how variations in fertility levels and family size influence the participation rates of married women in Jordan.

The measure of fertility levels most commonly used in studies of female labour force participation rates is the number of children ever-born. Relevant information available from the Jordan Fertility Survey of 1976 and summarised in Table 14 shows the mean number of children ever-born to women classified by pattern of work and the time that has elapsed since their first marriage. Four categories have been identified according to the pattern of work: (1) those who are currently working; (2) those who were working after marriage but are not currently working; (3) those who worked *only before* and *never since* marriage; and (4) those who have never worked.

Table 14: Mean number of children ever-born to ever-married women by years since marriage and by pattern of work[a]

| Pattern of work | Years since first marriage | | | | All cases |
	<5	5-14	15-24	>25	
Currently working	1.2	4.0	6.6	8.9	4.8
Worked after marriage- not now working	1.5	4.1	7.0	9.4	5.7
Worked *only* before marriage	1.1	4.3	7.4	9.4	4.8
Never worked	1.2	4.4	7.7	9.3	5.5

[a] Sample of 3,612 ever-married women.
Source: *Jordan Fertility Survey, 1976.*

Table 14 shows that within each category the mean number of children ever-born increases, as expected, with the number of years that have elapsed since first marriage. However, there are significant differences between the work categories. Taking all ever-married women, the mean number of children ever-born is highest for those who worked after marriage but are not currently working, that is, those who have withdrawn from the labour force at some stage after marriage. For those currently working and those who worked only before marriage the mean is lowest. A breakdown of the figures by number of years since marriage brings out the following significant features:

(1) Among those who have been married for less than five years, the mean number of children ever-born is highest for females who have withdrawn from the labour force some time after marriage. There is no significant difference between the remaining three categories.

(2) For those who have been married for more than five years, the mean number of children ever-born is lowest for currently working women and, in most cases, highest for those who have never worked.

(3) Irrespective of the time that has elapsed since marriage, the mean number of children ever-born is higher for those who have given up work at some stage after marriage than for the currently working.

The higher mean for those who have never worked than for the currently working indicates the expected inverse relationship between fertility and participation in economic activity. More significant, however, is that the means are higher for those women who have given up work some time after marriage than for those who are currently in the labour force. This suggests that a higher incidence of childbirth results in a withdrawal of married women from the labour force.

The relationship between female labour force participation and family size can be seen from variations in the mean number of living children by the mother's age and pattern of work. The figures given in Table 15 bring out the following significant features:

(1) Women who have never worked have, in each age-group, the highest number of living children.

(2) Except in the case of women aged 35-44 years, the mean number of living children is lowest for currently working women.

(3) Overall, women who have worked only before and never since marriage have on the average the least number of living children.

(4) Women who have worked after marriage but are not currently working have on the average a larger number of children than those currently working.

The higher average number of living children for mothers who have never worked than for the currently working indicates an inverse relationship between household size and labour force participation. Moreover, the higher average number of children reported by women who have worked up to some time after marriage than by the currently working shows that greater household responsibilities lead married women to withdraw from the labour force. However, for those who have worked only before and never since marriage, available evidence points to neither childbearing nor looking after a larger household as a significant factor in remaining out of the labour force. In their

Table 15: Mean number of living children by mother's age and pattern of work[a]

	Age of mother (years)				All ages
Pattern of work	<25	25-34	35-44	>45	
Currently working	2.0	4.1	6.8	6.8	4.8
Worked after marriage-not now working	2.2	4.1	6.5	7.6	5.2
Worked *only* before marraige	2.1	4.4	6.4	7.0	4.7
Never worked	2.4	5.2	7.4	7.8	5.4

[a] Covers 3,263 currently married mothers. Number of living children includes current pregnancy.

Source: *Jordan Fertility Survey, 1976.*

case it is the fact of marriage alone that underlies the decision to withdraw from the labour force.

It must be pointed out that the relationship between fertility and labour force participation is essentially two-way. While fertilify affects, as we have already seen, participation in economic activity, the desire and capability to take up a job are in turn likely to influence the decision to restrict family size. The Jordan Fertility Survey, 1976, collected some information on how the number of children desired by women varies according to their pattern of work. Table 16 shows the average total number of children women report- ing different patterns of work wish to have. The figures bring out three significant features: (1) The total number of children wanted on the average is highest for women who have never worked; (2) On the whole and for each category of women reporting the same number of currently living children (except for females with 6-8 children), those who have never worked or given up work since marriage desire a larger number of children than those currently working; (3) In each category of women reporting the same number of currently living children (except for females with 1-2 children), those who have given up work some time after marriage desire on the average fewer children than those currently working.

We can, therefore, say that female labour force participation tends to curtail the desire for larger families. More significantly the evidence indicates that an intention to participate in economic activity is associated with a desire for fewer children.[*] That women who have given up work some time after

*(The general hypothesis that female economic activity reduces desired and actual fertility has been found to hold in other studies. A cross-section study of 60 countries showed that a higher rate of female economic activity induced lower fertility levels (Kasarda, 1971). (See also analysis of data for 19 Latin American countries in Heer, and Turner, 1965).

Table 16: Mean total number of children wanted by currently married women by number of living children and pattern of work[a]

Pattern of work	Number of living children					All cases
	0	1-2	3-5	6-8	9+	
Currently working	3.9	3.9	5.7	7.9	8.0	6.0
Worked after marriage- not now working	3.5	3.9	4.9	7.5	7.8	5.9
Worked *only* before	4.3	4.8	5.8	7.3	9.0	6.1
Never worked	4.4	4.8	5.9	7.2	8.6	6.4

[a] Covers 3,458 currently married women. Number of living children includes current pregnancy.
Source: *Jordan Fertility Survey, 1976.*

marriage express a preference for fewer children than the currently working can best be explained by a persisting desire to rejoin the labour force which in all probability they feel they have been forced to withdraw from in order to bring up children.

The percentage of currently married 'fecund' mothers who want to have no more children (Table 17) supports the above findings. The proportion of women not wanting any more children is highest among those who have given up work some time after marriage. Overall the proportion of women not wanting any more children does not differ significantly between the currently

Table 17: Percentage of currently married 'fecund' mothers who want to have no more children by number of living children and pattern of work[a]

Pattern of work	Number of living children				All cases
	1-2	3-5	6-8	9+	
Currently working	12.0	42.8	51.3	87.9	39.8
Worked after marriage- not now working	21.0	52.8	68.0	77.7	53.1
Worked *only* before marriage	15.9	38.3	53.5	67.6	39.3
Never worked	8.7	34.5	64.9	78.4	44.1

[a] Covers 2,914 currently married 'fecund' mothers. Number of living children includes current pregnancy.
Source: *Jourdan Fertility Survey, 1976.*

working and those who have not worked since marriage. However, except in the case of women having 6-8 children, the proportion of women not wanting any more children is higher among the currently working than among those who have never worked. What is most significant is that among women who have given up work after marriage a much higher proportion want no more children than among the currently working. This, like their preference for fewer children, could also be explained by a desire to rejoin the labour force as soon as their existing children are old enough to permit this.

Husband's Occupation

The occupational groups reflect the social division of labour and, in the absence of information on household or husband's income, could also serve as a proxy for the economic status of the family. One could, therefore, expect that the occupational group to which the husband belongs would have some effect on the wife's decision to take up a paid job. Information on how female labour force participation varies according to the husband's occupation can be obtained from the Jordan Fertility Survey in which the following seven occupational categories are identified: Professional, technical and managerial; clerical workers; sales workers; service workers; skilled workers; unskilled workers; and, farmers and agricultural workers ('farmers' and 'agricultural workers' categorised separately in the Survey have been combined). While each occupational category comprises workers having different educational qualifications and incomes, it would not be unreasonable to expect this occupational classification 'to capture some socio-economic dimensions of the population studies' (Jordan, 1976: I, 21).

Table 18 shows female participation rates according to the occupational category of the husband and how the husband's occupation influence the wife's decision to give up work at marriage, or to take up a job after marriage. The participation rate is highest for wives of farmers and agricultural workers, and second highest for those in the highest professional category. The same is true for the percentage of women taking up work only after marriage. As to the percentage of working women giving up work at marriage, this is highest for those marrying workers in the highest professional category, and lowest for those marrying farmers and agricultural workers. The figures do not seem to suggest any direct association between the husband's occupation and the wife's work pattern. This may be due to the distortion resulting from the influence of the wives' educational standards on participation rates. Unfortunately female participation rates cross-classified by husband's occupation

Table 18: Female labour force participation by occupation of husband.

Husband's occupation	Percentage of women currently working	Percentage of women who took up work after marriage[a]	Percentage of working women who gave up work at marriage[b]
Professional, technical and managerial	17.1	10.5	79.9
Clerical workers	9.7	5.9	48.7
Sales workers	7.0	2.8	52.6
Service workers	7.8	5.7	60.8
Skilled workers	6.2	5.9	63.5
Unskilled workers	10.6	10.1	43.8
Agricultural workers and farmers	24.0	14.8	31.5

[a] Women who reported working *only* after marriage as a percentage of all those who reported as having never worked before marriage.
[b] Women who reported working only before and never since marriage as a percentage of all those who reported working before marriage.
Source: *Jordan Fertility Survey, 1976.*

and the level of education are not available. As there is, on the one hand, a positive relationship between the husband's occupation and the wife's level of education and, on the other, considerable variation in work attitudes according to the wife's educational attainment (Table 19), no firm conclusions can be drawn in respect of how the husband's occupation influences female participation in Jordan without such a cross-classification.

Migration and Urbanisation

The degree of urbanisation is known to have a considerable effect on female participation. While information on how participation rates vary according to migrant status is not available for Jordan, there is evidence that female participation rates have been higher in urban areas (Table 20).

The higher urban rates can be explained in terms of the foregoing analysis. First, cultural forces are likely to be weaker in urban areas than in rural areas. The cities and towns are generally less orthodox than the villages.

Table 19: Labour force participation, educational level and husband's occupation.

Husband's Occupation	Educational level						
	No schooling	Primary	Preparatory	Secondary	Institute	University	All levels
Professional, technical and managerial	27.0	25.1	16.4	20.7	5.2	5.6	100.0
Clerical workers	53.7	26.6	9.6	6.6	2.2	1.3	100.0
Sales workers	70.1	20.0	5.8	2.9	0.5	0.7	100.0
Service workers	77.4	16.4	3.1	2.3	0.3	0.5	100.0
Skilled workers	69.2	23.4	4.9	2.3	0.2	0.0	100.0
Unskilled workers	94.2	4.6	1.2	0.0	0.0	0.0	100.0
Agricultural workers and farmers	97.2	2.5	0.3	0.0	0.0	0.0	100.0
Percentage of women currently working	8.6	4.1	7.0	31.6	78.6	51.8	9.8
Percentage of working women who gave up work at marriage	56.8	69.5	55.6	32.1	0.0	22.7	51.9
Percentage of women who took up work after marriage	6.1	3.7	6.8	26.4	70.0	57.1	6.6

Source: *Jordan Fertility Survey, 1976.*

Table 20: Labour force participation rates in rural and urban areas, 1961-
1976.

	Labour force as percentage of population							
	Males				Females			
Age-group	1961		1976		1961		1976	
	Rural	Urban	Rural	Urban	Rural	Urban	Rural	Urban
15-19	60.0	52.2	31.6	28.7	2.6	5.9	2.0	4.0
20-24	91.0	88.5	81.9	79.8	2.9	9.9	10.7	25.5
25-29	94.6	93.0	97.4	96.2	2.0	6.0	5.9	21.0
30-39	94.8	93.7	97.2	97.7	1.7	4.3	1.0	8.0
40-49	93.8	90.1	93.0	93.7	1.5	3.8	0.9	3.6
50-59	87.3	73.9	84.2	82.7	0.9	2.9	1.0	1.8
60-64	76.5	52.4	56.4	54.5	0.6	1.6	0.9	1.1
15-64	85.0	80.0	73.5	73.3	2.0	5.7	3.2	9.8

Sources: *First Census of Population and Hosuing, 1961,* and *The Multi-purpose Household Survey, 1976.* For 1961, figures for urban areas include five cities and
towns — Ammar, Irbid, Salt, Karak and Ma'an.

Second, the incidence of education is known to be greater among urban
women.* Third, the urban population includes families who have migrated
from rural areas. Female members of such families are likely to accept low-
paid jobs more readily than they would in rural areas. This is because their
move to urban areas brings them out of their long-established social surround-
ings and as such they can cast away their fears of being looked down upon for
taking up paid work. Also, new migrants have fewer friends and relatives from
whom they can obtain financial support. This puts female members under
greater pressure to take up work in order to supplement the family income.
Such pressure is reinforced by the greater expenses in urban areas and the
delay which the male members of the migrant family face in getting an
adequately paid job.

*While the distribution of rural and urban population by educational attainment is not
available, the Multi-purpose Household Survey (1976) showed enrolment ratios to be
much higher in urban areas. For females aged 10-14 years, the enrolment ratios were
87.5 percent and 94.9 percent in rural and urban areas respectively. For females in age-
group 15-19, the ratio was 48.6 percent in rural areas and 66.2 percent in urban areas.

Conclusion and Policy Recommendations

This study shows that, in spite of a rising trend during the past two decades, female labour force participation rates in Jordan remain comparatively low. The low level of female participation in the labour force can be attributed to a spectrum of cultural, religious, demographic and economic factors. The main underlying cause of limited female economic activity appears to have been the socio-cultural set-up in which Islamic teachings, or rather their current interpretations, are a dominating influence. However, with the spread of education and increasing urbanisation, industrialisation and overall modernisation, Jordanian society appears to have been able to loosen the grip of traditional values and customs and an increasing number of Jordanian women have been participating in economic activity.

In addition to the cultural forces, this study identifies the responsibilities of child-bearing and household work and lack of education as the main deterrents to women's entry into the labour force. Sufficient evidence has been presented to merit the conclusion that higher fertility levels and a larger number of children to look after tend to force women out of the labour force. At the same time, women who consider themselves in a position of re-entering the labour force are found to be more in favour of restricting family size. That they do not succeed in having smaller families, can be attributed to a number of social and domestic factors including the shortage of family welfare programmes. Lack of education has been another significant obstacle to women's entry into the labour force. It is only with the attainment of at least secondary education that a woman's chances of entering the labour force appear to improve substantially. The prospects of being in the labour force are brightest for those who have had vocational training.

The main question to which we intend to address ourselves is whether or not it would be possible to increase female participation and how. On the basis of the past trends in prticipation rates, and the continuing spread of education among women, one can say with a considerable degree of confidence that Jordan is likely to witness an increase in female participation rates during this decade. However, it would be appropriate to introduce certain policy measures to speed and facilitate the achievement of higher levels of female participation. On the basis of this study the following measures can be suggsted as being most important:

(1) The mass media should be encouraged to propagate the positive role which women can and should play by participating in economic activity. The media sould also be used to change the negative attitude towards the taking up of paid work by women and to build up public opinion in

favour of it. It would be appropriate here to emphasise that traditions, particularly those which can be proved as being based on misguided Interpretations, can be modified, more so in the long-run, (see Ali, 1981).)

(2) Education facilities for girls should be expanded and girls should be provided with increased opportunities of pursuing courses in various specializations including technical and vocational training. Since women have stronger preferences for certain occupations and professions, greater attention should be paid to providing them with facilities for being trained in these lines. Similarly they should be encouraged to enroll for those skills in which manpower shortages are expected to occur.

(3) A national family welfare programme can be of considerable help to working women who wish to continue in the labour force after marriage or re-enter it as soon as possible after their children have grown up. The availability of family welfare facilities can go a long way in helping women to realise their desire for having a family size of their choice which as evidence suggests, is strongest among those who intend to participate in economic activity. To date family welfare activities in Jordan have remained limited and need to be expanded.

(4) The number of nurseries and childcare centres should be increased and their services provided to working women at reasonable rates. The availability of such facilities would enable women who would otherwise have to give up work to look after children to continue in their jobs.

(5) Recruitment rules should be so framed as to facilitate and encourage the re-entry into the labour force of women who are forced to withdraw from it due to the responsibilities of motherhood. For example, they should be allowed to rejoin without loss of status and seniority; and refresher programmes should be introduced to provide re-training.

(6) Women having children to look after are at times forced to withdraw from the labour force because they cannot work full-time. Special arrangements, therefore, should be made for allowing women to work part-time.

(7) Possibilities of sub-contracting work to women while they remain at home should be fully explored. This would enable not only those women who are forced to remain at home to look after children, but even those who cannot leave the house due to traditional values to participate in economic activity.

Bibliography

Ali, M., 1981. 'Saudis lift the veil on brides-to-be', *Jordan Times*. Amman: 7 April.
Azzam, H.T., 1979. *The Participation of Arab Women in the Labour Force: Development Factors and Policies*. (I.L.O., Population and Labour Policies Programme, Working Paper No. 80). Geneva.
Azzam, H.T. and Shaib, D., 1980. *The Women Left Behind: A Study of the Wives of Lebanese Migrant Workers in Oil-Rich Countries of the Region*. I.L.O., Population and Labour Policies – Regional Programme for the Middle East, Working Paper No. 3. Beirut.
Cain, G.G., 1966. *Married Women in the Labour Force*. University of Chicago Press.
Cohen, M., 1969. 'Married Women in the Labour Force: an Analysis of Participation Rates', *Monthly Labour Review*, vol. 92, no. 10, October.
Elizaga, J.C., 1974. 'The Participation of Women in the Labour Force of Latin America: Fertility and Other Factors', *International Labour Review*, vol. 10, nos. 5/6. May-June.
Farooq, G.M., 1972. 'An Aggregate Model of Labour Force Participation in Pakistan', *Developing Economies*, vol. 10, nos. 3. September.
Heer, D. and Turner, E.S., 1965. 'Areal Differences in Latin American Fertility', *Population Studies*, vol. 18, no. 3. March.
I.L.O., *Yearbook of Labour Statistics*, 1968, 1972, 1976, 1978, 1979, 1980.
Jaber, A.K.; Ati, S.A. and Gharaibeh, F., 1977. 'Conditions of Some Working Women in Jordan', in *Report of the Seminar on Population, Employment and Development*. National Planning Council and I.L.O. Amman: June.
Jordan, 1964. *First Census of Population and Housing, 1961*. The Hashemite Kingdom of Jordan, Department of Statistics.
–, 1977. *General Results of the Agricultural Census 1975*. The Hashemite Kingdom of Jordan, Department of Statistics.
–, 1981. *Industrial and Occupational Structure of the Labour Force: A Cross-Country Comparison*. National Planning Council, Department of Human Resources.
Jordan, 1979. *Jordan Fertility Survey 1976*. The Hashemite Kingdom of Jordan, Department of Statistics.
–, 1975. *The Labour Force Census 1975*. The Hashemite Kingdom of Jordan, Department of Statistics.
–, 1981. *Main Findings of Advance Tabulations: Housing and Population Census 1979*. The Hashemite Kingdom of Jordan, Department of Statistics. March.
–, 1977. *The Multi-Purpose Household Survey, 1976*. The Hashemite Kingdom of Jordan, Department of Statistics.
–, 1976. *National Fertility Survey in Jordan, 1972*. The Hashemite Kingdom of Jordan, Department of Statistics.
Kasarda, J.D., 1971. 'Economic Structure and Fertility: A Compartive Analysis', *Demography*, vol. 8, no. 3. August.
Nagi, M., 1971. *Labour Force and Employment in Egypt*. New York: Praeger.
Pakistan, 1963. *Census of Pakistan Population 1961*. Karachi: Government of Pakistan, Home Affairs Division.
Standing, G., 1976. 'Education and Female Participation in the Labour Force', *International Labour Review*, vol. 114, no. 3. March.
–, 1978. *Labour Force Participation and Development*. Geneva: I.L.O.
Standing, G. and Sheehan, G. (eds.), 1979. *Labour Force Participation in Low-Income Countries*. Geneva: I.L.O.
World Bank, 1980. *World Development Report, 1980*. Washington: August.

Chapter 6

Sex-Role Orientation of Arab University Students*

I. Lorfing and J. Abu Nasr**

The Research Problem and Objectives

Development planners in the Arab Middle East are increasingly giving serious attention to the integration of women in national development. Since 1954, a number of conferences and seminars have been held to discuss issues related to women and to study ways and means through which women can become active participants in the changing economic and social orders that characterize the region. Efforts have been made to promote the position of Arab women through legal enactments and socially-generated developmental changes. In most Arab countries, women were given the right to be educated, to vote and to be elected. Reforms to restrictive laws were also introduced, affecting women's status in matters of marriage and divorce. However, the low economic activity and the high fertility rate of women in the Arab countries (Youssef, 1974), indicate that interest in their integration and changes in the laws have not necessarily changed their role. The traditional role of women is confined to their being mothers and wives in a patriarchal family system. Their sphere of action is limited to their home; they are expected to be modest, obedient, and self-effacing. The persistence of these traditional values and attitudes among people of both sexes keeps women within the walls of their domestic world (Hillal, 1971; Keddie, 1978; Allawi, 1976), a situation that is incompatible with the demands of economic participation.

Little theoretical information and empirical evidence exist on the status and role of Arab women. However, available research (Prothro and Diab,

*This study was funded by a grant from the Ford Foundation to the Institute for Women's Studies in the Arab World.
**The authors wish to acknowledge the assistance of S. Saleh (American University in Cairo), H. Hammoud (Kuwait University) and L. Khoury (Beirut University College) in the preparation of this study.

1974; Allawi, 1976; Kandil and Kazemi, 1976; Abdel-Rahman, 1971; Al-Kottob, 1975; Accad, 1975) indicates that a change in attitudes towards traditional sex-role orientation is noticeable among Arab women, especially among the young, the educated and the economically productive.

The present chapter capitalizes on previous research in the area of sex-roles and attempts to provide empirical evidence from three Arab countries that could substantiate some of the results obtained. The objective of this investigation is to measure the attitudes of Arab university students of both sexes towards sex-role orientation in today's Arab society. The direction and dimension of attitude change from the traditional to the non-traditional axis will be assessed for each sex in the light of certain personal and family variables.

Methodology

For the purpose of this study a questionnaire was designed which consisted of several open-ended questions on issues related to sex-roles, such as: wife-mother role, husband-father role, husband-wife relations, women's employment and economic independence and women's access to education. For the choice of questions, the investigators relied heavily on already published research (Kandil and Kazem, 1976; Abdel-Rahman, 1971; Al Kottob, 1975; Accad, 1975). The language of the questionnaire was classical Arabic, a language common to all respondents. The questionnaire was tested for content validity and scoring technique reliability. It was administered in regularly-scheduled classes during the Spring of 1979.

The response to each question was ranked from 1 to 3, where non-traditional responses received a score of 1, transitional a score of 2, and traditional a score of 3. The direction and dimension of attitude change is assessed by the mean score of each respondent. The mean score was calculated on the basis of responses to each item. High mean scores indicate traditionalism, and low mean scores non-traditionalism.

The dependent variable in the study is the mean sex-role orientation score of the respondent on all items of the questionnaire. The independent variables were defined as follows: (1) Father's occupation: professional and administrative, owner or manager of commercial enterprise, clerical, skilled, owner or manager of commercial enterprise, clerical, skilled, unskilled and agricultural worker, unemployed or retired; (2) mother's occupation was classified as working or housewife (mother's occupations were not classified by categories due to the low percentage of working mothers in Kuwait); (3) Father's and mother's education: university, high school, elementary, no education; (4) religion: Christian-Moslem, other; (5) age of student, and class at university.

The analytical scheme examined the data on the three levels: first, the significance of male-female differences with respect to sex-role orientation; second, the relative influence of each independent variable on the dependent variable; finally, the relative power of each combination of independent variables in explaining the variance in sex-role attitude scores.

The Sample

The total sample consisted of 166 males and 267 female Arab university students from Lebanon, Egypt and Kuwait. Students were selected from the following universities: Beirut University College (BUC), American University of Beirut (AUB), University of Kuwait (UK), and American University in Cairo (AUC). The sample was incidental and included students with at least two years of university education. The ratio of females to males in each country sample ranged between 1.5 and 1.7. Over 60 percent of the respondents were Moslems and less than 25 years of age. The majority of the fathers and mothers of the Lebanese and Egyptian samples had at least high-school education compared to 28 percent for the Kuwaitis' fathers and 9 percent for the mothers. In line with high educational levels, the most frequently-reported occupations of the fathers of the Lebanese and Egyptian students were: professionals, managers, administrators and businessmen, whereas in the case of the Kuwaiti sample, the majority were either businessmen or employees. As for mother's work experience, 69 percent of the Lebanese and 57 percent of the Egyptian respondents indicated that the mothers have worked or are working, compared to 14 percent for Kuwaitis. The familial characteristics of our sample reveal that the Lebanese and Egyptian students attending BUC, AUB and AUC come from higher middle-class backgrounds, while the Kuwaitis seem to come from lower socio-economic strata (see Table 1).

Table 1: Characteristics of the student population

Characteristics	Lebanon		Kuwait		Egypt	
	N	%	N	%	N	%
Sex						
Males	67	40	39	36	60	38
Females	99	60	68	64	100	62

contd.

Table 1 (contd.)

Characteristics	Lebanon		Kuwait		Egypt	
	N	%	N	%	N	%
Class at university						
2nd year	53	32	11	10	5	3
3rd year	66	40	66	62	99	62
4th year	47	28	30	28	56	35
Age						
19-21	94	57	57	53	112	70
22-24	55	33	30	28	41	26
25+	17	10	20	19	7	4
Religion						
Christians	49	30	2	2	35	22
Moslems	100	60	105	98	120	75
Other	17	10	–	–	5	3
Father's education						
University	68	41	2	2	142	89
High school	65	39	28	26	10	6
Elementary	21	13	24	22	1	1
No education	6	4	46	43	–	–
No answer	6	3	7	7	7	4
Mother's education						
University	35	21	1	1	73	46
High school	78	47	9	8	77	48
Elementary	34	20	26	24	4	2
No education	13	8	5	5	6	4
No answer	6	4	5	5	6	4
Father's occupation						
Professional and administrative	21	13	1	1	79	50
Commercial-owners	94	57	39	36	53	33
Chemical and skilled	31	18	32	30	7	4
Unskilled and agricultural	–	–	5	5	–	–
Unemployed and retired	4	3	11	10	5	3
No answer	16	9	19	18	16	10
Mother's occupation						
Housewife	50	31	92	86	68	43
Working	116	69	15	14	92	57

Findings and Discussion

The findings from Lebanon, Kuwait and Egypt brought out certain facts and relationships concerning the direction and dimension of change in the attitudes of Arab university students towards the role of women in contemporary Arab societies. The data revealed that the sample was in a transitional stage, half way between traditionalism and non-traditionalism and that women are significantly less traditional in their outlook than men. These results are in line with findings of previous studies in the Arab world where males were found to be more supportive of traditional norms than females with respect of women's role (Stino, 1976; Dodd, 1974; Takla, 1978; Accad, 1974). As indicated in Table 2, the mean sex-role orientation scores for both sexes cluster around the score of 2, which is considered a transitional score.

Table 2: Summary table presenting sex-role orientation mean scores and 95% confidence intervals for the true population mean by sex and country.

Mean Scores and Sex	Lebanon	Kuwait	Egypt
Males:			
Mean scores	2.004	2.300	2.001
95% confidence interval	1.902, 2.106	2.190, 2.420	1.887, 2.115
Females:			
Mean Scores	1.782	2.140	1.801
95% confidence interval	1.702, 1.862	2.040, 2.230	1.731, 1.871

However, certain differences between the countries are noticeable with respect to the dimension of change. The 95 percent intervals of the population means of each sex in the different countries show that Lebanese and Egyptian males were less traditional than the Kuwaitis, although the three samples can be classified as transitional. As for female students, mean scores indicate that the Lebanese group was the least traditional, followed by the Egyptian and then the Kuwaitis. In both instances the true population mean was smaller than 2, whereas that of Kuwaiti females was over 2. When individual attitude scores were analyzed in relation to personal and familial factors, the effect of each independent variable on sex-role orientation of respondents was measured by regression coefficients for each sex separately (see Table 3).

Data in Table 3 reveal that none of the personal variables of age, class at university or religion are significantly related to the attitude scores of both sexes in the Lebanese, Egyptian of Kuwaiti samples. Some family variables: mother's education, mother's work experiences and father's education, are found to be positively related to sex-role orientation scores.

Table 3: Summary table showing the simple regression coefficients of the studied variables indicating their effect on sex-role orientation scores, by country and sex.

Country & Sex	Simple Regression Coefficients*						
	Father's Education	Mother's Education	Father's Occupation	Mother's Work Experience	Age	Class at University	Religion
Lebanon:							
Males	.040	-.055	-.026	.004	.042	-.085	.040
Females	-.068	.103*	.073	.001	.021	-.011	NS**
Kuwait:							
Males	.114*	-.072	.026	-.31	.084	.018	-.081
Females	-.068	.121*	.005	NS**	-.003	-.012	.326
Egypt:							
Males	-.057	-.099	-.008	.036*	.019	-.186	.035
Females	-.128	.053	.055	NS**	-.005	.055	-.019

*Statistically significant at the .05 level.
**The variable has an insignificant level of inclusion and, therefore, is deleted from the analysis.

Mother's education was found to be significantly related to the attitude scores of the Lebanese and Kuwaiti female students. This positive relationship between liberal attitudes of daughters and mothers' levels of education was also found in other studies, indicating that the effect of mothers' education is more noticeable in the case of female children (Hammoud, 1980). The reason for the absence of any significant relationship in the Egyptian sample may be accounted for by the homogeneity of mothers' education, where 95 percent have high school education or better.

Findings also indicate that in the Kuwaiti sample, fathers' education is strongly and positively related to sons' sex-role orientation. This observation substantiates previous results on the subject, which state that fathers' educational achievement is more effective in the case of male children (Hammoud, 1980; Tohmeh, 1978). However, this relationship did not prove to be significant in the case of the present Lebanese and Egyptian samples, a situation that could be explained by the overrepresentation of fathers in the higher educational levels (80 percent in Lebanon and 95 percent in Egypt). Fathers' occupation does not show any significant relationship to sons' and daughters' sex-role attitudes.

In the case of mothers, work experience does not show any strong relationship with children's attitudes, except in the case of the Egyptian male students, where mothers' work experience was found to have a significant and positive effect on attitudes towards sex-roles, a finding supported by previous results (Tohmeh, 1978; Tangri, 1972). The absence of such a relationship in the Lebanese and Kuwait sample could be explained in terms of levels of inclusion, referring to the number of observations and the type of occupation of mothers. The majority of Egyptian mothers were professionals.

In the three countries studied, family variables of fathers' education, mothers' education, fathers' occupation and mothers' work experiences contribute more to the explanation of variance among females than males, and more than personal variables of age, class at university and religion. Family variables were found to account more substantially for the variations among the Kuwaiti and Egyptian males, 0.28 and 0.14 percent, respectively, than among the males in Lebanon and the females in the three countries. The same pattern is found for personal variables, which contribute more in terms of variance in sex-role orientation scores of the Kuwaiti and Egyptian males than of the Kuwaiti and Egyptian females or of both Lebanese males and females.

Table 4 shows the relative power of each combination of independent variables, family and personal, in explaining the variance in sex-role attitude scores.

Table 4: Summary table showing the percentage of variation in sex-role orientation scores explained by familial and personal factors, by sex and country.

	Lebanon		Kuwait		Egypt	
Factors	Males	Females	Males	Females	Males	Females
Familial	.02	.08	.28	.09	.14	.04
Personal	.05	.03	.09	.04	.06	.001

Mothers' Education

The partial regression coefficients for mothers' education in the case of males and females indicate that when the other three variables, fathers' education and fathers' and mothers' occupation, were controlled for, the effect of mothers' education on children's attitudes was increased only in the case of Egyptian males and Kuwaiti females. The explanatory power of this variable, mothers' education, shows that it is a stronger determinant of sex-role orientation for women than it is for men, and this holds true for the three countries. In the case of women, the relative share of variance explained by mothers' education in relation to the total explanatory power of all the family variables was highest for Kuwaitis, followed by the Lebanese and then the Egyptians. In the case of men, this contribution drops in all three countries. These results corroborate previous findings on females samples, reporting that mothers' educational level is a strong determinant of the sex-role orientation of daughters (Mason and Bumpass, 1975; Meir, 1972).

Fathers' Education

The impact of fathers' education on sex-role attitudes, when confounding effects of other family variables are controlled is more pronounced in the case of males than in the case of females for the Lebanese and the Kuwaiti samples, while this relationship is reversed for the Egyptian group. The percentage increment brought by fathers' education to the variation in sex-role attitudes of males, as explained by mothers' education and mothers' and fathers' occupations, is highest for Kuwait, substantial for Lebanon and almost negligible for Egypt. In the case of females, the results of the Egyptian sample contradict previous findings (Tohmeh, 1978), reporting that fathers' education has more effect on the sex-role orientation of males than females. The very weak explanatory power of fathers' education in the case of the Egyptian sample could be attributed to the homogeneity in educational achievement of students' fathers, where 89 percent of them are university graduates.

Fathers' Occupation

The relationship between fathers' occupation and children's attitudes was slightly affected when the other family variables, mothers' education, fathers' education and mothers' work experience, were controlled for in the three countries. However, the relative portion of variance explained by fathers' occupation in relation to the total explanatory power of family variables proved to be more substantial in the case of females in both the Lebanese and the Egyptian samples. In the case of males, the explanatory power of this variable was highest for the Lebanese, followed by Kuwaitis, and lowest for the Egyptians.

Mothers' Work Experience

Mothers' work experience when analyzed in conjunction with the other family variables, proved to have more explanatory power in the case of males than females in Lebanon, Egypt and Kuwait. However, in Egypt, it proved to be the highest contributor to the explanation of variance among males. In general, the relative share of mothers' work experience in the total explanatory power of the familial factors was systematically higher for males than females in the three countries.

Class at University

Class at university was not found to be significantly related to sex-role attitdues of respondents. However, data reveal that the length of stay at the university was inversely related to liberal attitudes for Lebanese of both sexes and for Kuwaiti women and Egyptian men.

The percentage of variance explained by class at university when the other personal variables were controlled for is higher for Lebanese and Egyptian males than for females. In Kuwait, this relationship is reversed and the relative share of this variable to the total explanatory power of the combination of the three personal variables is higher for women.

Age

Age of respondents did not prove to be a significant determinant of sex-role attitudes. However, simple regression coefficients indicate that younger Kuwaiti and Egyptian female students were more liberal than older ones, whereas in the remaining group this relationship was reversed. The amount of variation attributed to age of respondents was substantial only for Lebanese females and Kuwaiti males, when analyzed in conjunction with other personal variables.

Religion

Although religion was not significantly related to sex-role orientation of respondents, it was found to account for more of the variation explained by personal factors for the Lebanese males and the Kuwaiti females, whereas its explanatory power is very small for the remaining sample. Christian Lebanese and Egyptian males and Kuwaiti females were found to be more liberal than Moslem Kuwaiti male students and Egyptian female students.

Summary and Conclusion

The results of the present collaborative study indicate without doubt that changes are occurring in Arab society. The attitude of Arab university students of both sexes towards sex-role orientation was found to be (transitional, thus suggesting that the value system of society is being questioned. This finding is in line with research on sex-role orientation in other cultures.

Among the determining factors, familial and personal variables, namely, father's education, mother's education, father's occupation, mother's occuaption and age, sex, religion, and class at university, gave some insight into the factors that affect these attitudes. Father's and mother's education, father's occupation and mother's work experience brought some explanation to the total variation among sex-role orientation scores. However, the percentage of variation explained was not consistent among the different countries and between the sexes. Like family variables, the investigated personal variables explain little about the formation of these attitudes.

What emerges from these findings is, first, that sex is the best predictor of sex-role attitudes in general, and that the investigated sets of familial and personal variables explain a small part of the variation in sex-role attitudes. The question arises as to what are the other factors that contribute most to the variation in sex-role orientation? It should be remembered that college students represent a small and special segment of Arab society and that they are a homogeneous group. What is needed is a larger and a more representative sample of Arab society, whose heterogeneous background may reveal a greater variability in sex-role orientation and where the investigated variables may carry greater explanatory power. More recent research in the field pointed out the importance of attitudinal variables (Tohmeh, 1978) in the study of sex-role orientation. Moreover, exploratory studies in the areas of socialization of children, self-image and role perception in relation to sex-role attitudes are needed for a more comprehensive study of the factors that affect the formation of sex-role attitudes in the Arab world.

Bibliography

Abdel Kader, S., 1973. *The Status of Egyptian Women, 1900-1973.* Cairo: Social Research Center.

Abdel-Rahman, S., 1971. *Dirāsat Awda'h Wa Ittijahāt Al Maraāt Al Kuwaitia.* (Studies of the Status and Attitudes of Kuwaiti Woman). Kuwait: Jamiāt Al Nahda Al Arabia Al Nissaia (in Arabic).

Accad-Sursock, R., 1974. 'La Femme Libanaise de la Tradition à la Modernité'. *Travaux et Jours* 52: 17-38.

Alawi, A., 1976. *Woman's Work, Trends and Motives in The Role of The Jordanian Woman:* Second Symposium on Manpower Development. Amman: April 4-7.

Al Kotob, I., 1975. *Ittijahāt Al Fatāt Al-Jamiiah Al Khalijia Nahou Ba'ad Al Qadāya Al*

Ijtimahiah Al Qaoumiah. (Attitudes of Female University Students Towards Societal and National Issues). Al Jamiah Al Thakafia Al Ijtimahiah Al Nissaia. First Regional Seminar of the women of the Gulf. Kuwait: April 21 (in Arabic).

Badr el Din, A., 1965. 'The Arab Working Woman as Seen in Our University Girls'. *Arab Observer,* July.

Bashour, M., 1980. 'Arab Women and Education'. Institute for Women's Studies in the Arab World. *Monograph* 2: 63-90.

Bayer, A., 1975. 'Sexist Students in American Colleges: A Descriptive Note'. *Journal of Marriage and the Family* 37: 391-339.

Beck, L. and Keddie, N., 1978. *Women in the Muslim World.* Cambridge, Massachussetts: Harvard University Press.

Brogan, D. and Kutner, N., 1976. 'Measuring Sex Role Orientation: A Normative Approach'. *Journal of Marriage and the Family* 38: 31-40.

Burlin, F.D., 1976. 'The Relationship of Parental Education and Maternal Work and Occupational Status to Occupational Aspiration in Adolescent Females'. *Journal of Vocational Behavior* 9: 99-104.

Dodd, p., 1974. 'Concerning the Effect of Religious Affiliation on Woman's Role in Middle-Eastern Arab Society'. *Journal of Comparative Family Studies* 4: 212-227.

–, 1973. 'Family Honor and the Forces of Change in Arab Society'. *International Journal of Middle East Studies* 4: 40-54.

–, 1968. 'Youth and Women's Emancipation in the UAR'. *The Middle East Journal* 22: 159-173.

Duberman, L. and Azumi, K., 1975. 'Sexism in Nepal'. *Journal of Marriage and the Family* 37: 1013-1021.

Ferber, M. and Huber, J., 1975. 'Sex of Student and Instructor: A Study of Student Bias'. *American Journal of Sociology* 80: 949-963.

Ghandour, L., 1968. 'The Relationship of Attitues to Social Class in Beirut, Lebanon'. M.A. thesis, American University of Beirut (unpublished).

Haavio-Mannila, E., 1972. 'Sex-Role Attitudes in Finland, 1966-1970'. *Journal of Social Issues* 28: 93-109.

Haikal, A., 1971. *Some Managerial Problems of Female Employment in the UAR.* M.A. Thesis, the American University in Cairo (unpublished).

Hilal, J., 1971. 'The Management of Male Dominance in Traditional Arab Culture: A Tentative Model'. *Civilization* 21: 85-95.

Ibrahim, S. and Hopkins, N. (eds.), 1977. *Arab Society in Transition.* Cairo: The American University in Cairo Press.

Kandil, A. and Kazemi, M., 1976. *Ittijah al Fatat al Muta'allima Nahou Amal Al Mara'a.* (Attitude of the Educated Girl Towards the Work of Woman). Cairo: Angelo Press (in Arabic).

Mason, K. and Bumpass, L., 1975. 'U.S. Women's Sex-Role Ideology, 1970'. *American Journal of Sociology* 80: 1212-1219.

–, 1976. "Change in U.S. Women's Sex-Role Attitudes, 1964-1974'. *American Sociological Review* 41: 573-596.

Meghdessian, S., 1980. *The Status of the Arab Women – A Bibliography.* London: Mansell.

Meier, H.C., 1972. 'Mother-Centerdness and College Youth's Attitudes Toward Social Equality for Women'. *Journal of Marriage and the Family* 34: 115-121.

Myntti, C., 1974. 'Changing Roles in Five Beirut Households'. In James Allman (ed.), *Women's Status and Fertility in the Muslim World.* New York: Praeger Publishers.

Nath, I., 1978. 'Education and Employment Among Kuwaiti Women'. In Beck, L. and Keddie N. (eds.), *Women in the Muslim World.* Cambridge Massachussetts: Harvard University Press.

Nelson, C., 1976. 'Social Change in Sexual Identity in Contemporary Egypt'. In De Vos, G. (ed.), *Response to Change.* New York: Van Nostrand.

Parelius, A., 1975. 'Emerging Sex-Role, Attitudes, Expectations and Strains Among College Women'. *Journal of Marriage and the Family* 37: 146-153.

Prothro, E. and Diab, L., 1974. *Changing Family Patterns in the Arab East*. Beirut: American University of Beirut.

République Libanaise, Ministère du Plan, Direction Centrale de la Statistique, 1972. *L'Enquête par sondage sur la population active au Liban*. Beyrouth.

Saleh, S., 1972. 'Women in Islam, their Status in Religious and Traditional Culture'. *International Journal of Sociology of the Family* 1: 1-8.

—, 1972. 'Women in Islam, their Role in Religious and Traditional Culture'. *International Journal of Sociology of the Family* 2: 193-201.

Smock, A.C. and Youssef, N., 1975. 'The Changing Roles and Status of Women in Egypt'. In Smock, A. (ed.), *Women and Society: an International and Comparative Perspective*. Ford Foundation.

Stino, L., 1976. *The Working Wife: Attitudes, Perceptions and Role Expectations of Five Male Cairenes*. Thesis, American University in Cairo (unpublished).

Takla, S., 1978. *The Relationship between Socio-economic class, Sex-role attitudes, and Internal-External Orientation of Daughters of Working versus Non-Working Mothers*. Thesis, American University of Beirut (unpublished).

Tangri, S.S., 1972. 'Determinants of Occupational Role Innovation Among College Women'. *Journal of Social Issues* 28: 177-199.

Tohme, A., 1978. 'Sex-Role Orientation: An Analysis of Structural and Attitudinal Predictors'. *Journal of Marriage and the Family* 40: 341-345.

UNESCO, 1974. *Report on the Relationship between Educational Opportunities and Employment Opportunities for Women in Lebanon*. Paris.

Weitz, S., 1977. *Sex-Roles, Biological, Psychological and Social Foundations*. New York: Oxford University Press.

Youssef, N., 1978. 'The Status and Fertility Patterns of Muslim Women'. In Beck, L. and Keddie, L. (eds.), *Women in the Muslim World*. Cambridge Massachussetts: Harvard University Press.

—, 1974. 'Women and Work in Developing Societies'. *Institute of International Studies*. Berkeley: University of California.

DA

RET